Merry Christmas and a Happy New Year

Christian enlightenment and encouragement for a special season

Timothy Cross

Day One

© Day One Publications 2020
First Edition 2020

British Library Cataloguing in Publication Data available

ISBN 978-1-84625-680-6

Published by Day One Publications
Ryelands Road, Leominster, HR6 8NZ

☎ 01568 613 740
FAX: 01568 611 473
email—sales@dayone.co.uk
web site—www.dayone.co.uk

Designed by Kathryn Chedgzoy and printed by 4edge

To Frank and June:
'A friend loves at all times,
and a brother is born for adversity'
(Proverbs 17:17).

Contents

Foreword

It gives me great pleasure to highly commend Timothy Cross's book *Merry Christmas and a Happy New Year!* With its great mixture of strong Bible doctrine, beautiful poems and wonderfully biblical hymns, this is a book that is thoroughly Christ-exalting and God-glorifying. I have read several books authored by Timothy and they all, together with this one, have one major feature that is thoroughly refreshing and passionately powerful: they all bleed the Bible. There is not much more you can ask from a Christian author. He continually and powerfully points people to His blessed Lord and Saviour, Jesus Christ, and does so by weaving together solid biblical doctrine on every page.

This would be a great gift for all believers, including Sunday school teachers, elders and pastors, and even for those who may be outside the faith. It is a book that gives hope, encouragement and instruction, and coming in a year of the coronavirus pandemic, it is just what we all need to guide us and lovingly propel us into a brand-new year, all for God's glory and our good.

By His grace,

Bill Hoving

Co-pastor, Cornwall Street Baptist Church

Cardiff, Wales

Preface

Christmas and the New Year are special occasions on the calendar which give us warm and lasting memories. They are celebrated in both the sacred and the secular worlds, and are the cause of many a party.

If Christmas and the New Year are marked by people in general, how much greater reason have Christians to celebrate these two occasions! Christmas marks the birth of Christ and His coming into the world to accomplish our salvation. Christmas is thus a major milestone in the story of redemption. Likewise with the New Year. When the old year is behind us and the new year is before us, it is surely time to stop and thank God for His goodness and faithfulness to us, and to entrust Him with whatever He has in store for us in the future:

> 'Tis Jesus, the First and the Last,
> Whose Spirit shall guide us safe home;
> We'll praise Him for all that is past,
> And trust Him for all that's to come.[1]

Yet Christmas and the New Year are not always times of unalloyed joy. When a loved one has died, their absence seems all the more acute at Christmastime. Facing a new year can then be intimidating—it can seem like a mountain which is far bigger than we are, yet we have no choice but to climb it. How we need the grace of God!

I send out the following chapters praying that they will be a means of divine grace. They are messages which I trust will bring Christian encouragement and enlightenment for Christmas and the New Year. The key to both seasons is the Lord Jesus Christ. Knowing Him as our Saviour and Friend is the key to a happy Christmas and a joyful New Year. His grace will most surely keep pace with whatever we face! The Lord Jesus Christ, though, is more than just the key to a merry Christmas and a happy New Year. He is and will be the proven key to a happy life, a happy death and a happy eternity.

May the Lord bless you and draw near to you as you read.

Timothy Cross

Cardiff, Wales

Merry Christmas and a Happy New Year!

Part 1:
A merry Christmas

Celebrating a celebration?

The story is told of a man who decided that, to mark his retirement, having worked in the same company for over forty years, he would throw a party for his colleagues, friends and family. He hired a hall, booked a jazz band, contacted some outside caterers and sent out invitations. On the appointed day, a great crowd descended on the hall, and as the evening wore on, they began to really 'whoop it up'. Strangely, though, the host himself did not turn up! He couldn't face it. Sadly, the nearer he got to retirement, the more depressed he got. It was something to do with thoughts of growing old, and of being no more economic use. But this didn't stop the party-goers from enjoying themselves! They ate and drank; they laughed; they enjoyed a great camaraderie—so much so, that they completely missed the original purpose of the party.

The same can be true of us at Christmas. We can get so carried away with the presents, fun and festivities that we miss the main reason for it all. Many do not give even a thought to the main reason for Christmas, yet this does not prevent them celebrating. They too 'whoop it up'—but they are really just 'celebrating a celebration'.

On the first Christmas night, a message from heaven to earth was given. It is recorded in Luke 2:11 and it captures in a nutshell the real 'reason for the season' of Christmas. The verse reads: 'To you is born this day in the city of David a Savior, who is Christ the Lord.' Keeping this verse in mind will surely enable us to celebrate Christmas and not just celebrate a celebration.

Note the following from this verse:

The place

'To you is born this day *in the city of David.*' The 'city of David' refers to the 'little town of Bethlehem' where Christ was born. Bethlehem sets Christmas in time and space. Here we are dealing with history, not mythology. If you have the means, you can fly to Tel Aviv. From there you can take a coach to Jerusalem. From Jerusalem you can take a bus five or so miles to the south-west, and you will arrive in . . . Bethlehem. Christ was born in this exact location, as the prophet Micah had foretold (see Micah 5:2). His birth was so significant that it divided our calendar into the eras of BC and AD. Christmas concerns an event which really happened, in time and space.

The person

Our verse tells us that none other than 'Christ the Lord' was born in Bethlehem. He is the One at the heart of Christmas. 'Christ' is a title, not a name. It means 'the anointed one' or 'Messiah'. In Jesus, the longed-for Messiah, promised by God, arrived. In Old Testament times, prophets, priests and kings were all anointed with oil at the outset of their ministries. It symbolized their being set apart by God and endowed with His Holy Spirit. As *the* anointed one, Jesus combined the threefold role of prophet, priest and king in His one person.

Notice that He is also described as 'the Lord'. This is a title for God Himself. The uniqueness of the Christian faith stems from the uniqueness of the Christ of the Christian faith. He is

God! Christians contend for the absolute deity of the Christ revealed in the Bible. Jesus is 'Emmanuel, God with us'. He is God in the flesh, for 'in him the whole fulness of deity dwells bodily' (Col. 2:9).

The purpose

Luke 2:11 actually takes us to the heart of the heart of Christmas when it says, 'To you is born this day in the city of David a *Savior*.' Christ's coming into the world to be our Saviour therefore is the divine purpose behind Christmas. Christ's coming into the world to be our Saviour also encapsulates the very essence of the Christian gospel. 'Christ Jesus came into the world to save sinners' (1 Tim. 1:15). 'You shall call his name Jesus, for he will save his people from their sins' (Matt. 1:21).

The word 'Saviour' means a rescuer or deliverer. This begs the question: from what does Christ save? The answer of the Bible is that Christ saves sinners from the divine condemnation they deserve for their sins. He saves us from the wrath of God. He saves us from the very flames of hell. Our greatest need is for a Saviour, for by nature we are all sinners, and thus liable to the wrath of God. The gospel proclaims that in Christ alone we find the only Saviour for our need. This takes us from Christ's cradle to His cross, for Christ was born to die. Salvation was procured, not by the birth of Christ, but by His death—when, thirty-three years later, He offered up His sinless life as an atoning sacrifice for the sins of others, 'that whoever believes in him should not perish but have eternal life' (John 3:16).

The purpose of Christmas? It was salvation. Jesus came to execute God's eternal plan of salvation. He came to be our Saviour.

The pertinence

'To *you* is born this day in the city of David a Savior.' God's salvation reaches real people. The 'you' here refers to some shepherds who were going about their business in the fields surrounding Bethlehem. On the first Christmas, Almighty God graciously intervened in their lives. But the verse has a wider application. God's offer of salvation still extends to sinners today. The gospel invitation is made 'to *you*'.

Jesus is a Saviour to receive. 'The free gift of God is eternal life in Christ Jesus our Lord' (Rom. 6:23). Have you received Him? You certainly need Him. And you may still receive Him, for He never turns away anyone when they confess that they are a lost sinner and cast themselves on Him for salvation.

'To *you* is born this day in the city of David a Savior, who is Christ the Lord.' Here is the greatest Christmas present you can or ever will receive. The salvation of God in Christ is a gift to enjoy in life, in death and for all eternity.

> O holy child of Bethlehem,
> Descend to us, we pray;
> Cast out our sin and enter in,
> Be born in us today.
> We hear the Christmas angels
> The great glad tidings tell;

O come to us, abide with us,
Our Lord Immanuel![1]

Reflect on these points

1. *We can get so carried away with the presents, fun and festivities of Christmas that we miss the main reason for it all, and are really just 'celebrating a celebration'.*

2. *From what does Christ save? The answer of the Bible is that Christ saves sinners from the wrath of God. He saves us from the very flames of hell.*

3. *Jesus is a Saviour to receive. And God's offer of salvation still extends to sinners today. The gospel invitation is made 'to you'. Have you received Him?*

God in a manger

Our familiarity with the first Christmas scene can easily blunt us to its staggering wonder. Luke 2:12 records the infant Christ as 'lying in a manger'. Think of that: here is condescension and humiliation of the highest degree, for here is the eternal Son of God—the One through whom God made all things, the One who is dependent on nobody—now lying in a manger as a helpless baby, completely dependent on others for support. A well-known carol is right when it states 'Lo, within a manger lies He who built the starry skies.'[1] A less-well-known carol likewise runs:

> The eternal Word, who built the earth and skies,
> Takes on Him flesh, and in a manger lies;
> In that dear Babe of Bethlehem I see
> My God, contracted to a span for me.[2]

Why, though, at the first Christmas, did the eternal Son of God lie in a trough normally used for animal feed? We can answer the question from two perspectives. There is a human answer to the question and there is also a divine answer.

The human answer

Luke 2:7 tells us that Mary 'laid him in a manger, because there was no place for them in the inn'. Bethlehem was crowded. Accommodation was at a premium, as people returned to their towns of origin to be enrolled for taxation purposes. Perhaps the proprietor of the inn had quibbles about giving hospitality to a woman who was evidently about to give birth. But think a little deeper. Prophecy was being fulfilled, and the divine plan of salvation was being worked out. A virgin had conceived and given birth to Emmanuel. Almighty God had taken upon Himself human flesh. The Messiah had arrived. The angels of heaven were celebrating . . . but earth seemed indifferent. There was no great reception for the Saviour. He was crowded out. Folk went on their earth-bound course as normal. 'He was in the world, and the world was made through him, yet the world knew him not' (John 1:10).

Things do not seem to have changed much, even these two thousand or so years later. How many who celebrate Christmas truly celebrate the Christ of Christmas? How many who welcome the 'festive season' have given a welcome to the eternal Saviour? Christ can still get crowded out, ignored, neglected and even rejected, to the eternal peril of a person's soul.

> The crowded inn, like sinners' hearts—
> O ignorance extreme!
> For other guests of various sorts
> Had room; but none for Him.[3]

We need not be unduly pessimistic, however, as the Bible teaches God's effectual calling and irresistible grace. He will most surely save His people. He will most certainly break down all the barriers and draw His people to Christ. No obstacle is too great for omnipotence! When God's Holy Spirit has been at work in the human soul, there will always be room for Jesus! Just as Christ was born miraculously of the Holy

Spirit, so every Christian has similarly been reborn of the same Holy Spirit of God.

The divine answer

The divine answer to the question why Christ lay in a manger is given many times in the New Testament. For instance, 1 Timothy 1:15 tells us simply and succinctly that 'Christ Jesus came into the world to save sinners.' The Son of God, then, was born to save sinners. He lived to save sinners, and eventually He died and rose again to save sinners. We are all sinners, worthy of God's wrath. But Christ came into the world to save us from God's wrath. This is the gospel—the truly 'Good News' that transcends Christmastime.

One way in which the Bible describes God's judgement is by the formidable term 'the second death'. Christ died that sinners who believe in Him might be saved from the second death. Hebrews 9:22 states that 'without the shedding of blood there is no forgiveness of sins'. Hence the eternal, immortal God took upon Himself our flesh and blood, and laid down His sinless life for sinners at Calvary, so that He might bestow upon us the gift of eternal life. His precious blood was shed there for the sinner's forgiveness.

So Christ's birth—His lying in a manger—was all part of God's great eternal plan of redemption. God Himself sent His only Son into the world so that His people could be saved—reconciled to God—and enjoy God's fellowship for all eternity. Almighty God has His plan of redemption. And if your faith is in the Christ of Bethlehem who became the Christ of Calvary, you have been embraced in God's gracious redemption. One day you will see Christ face to face and rejoice evermore that He was born for you at Bethlehem and died for you at Calvary to pay the price for your sins.

There is a well-known Christmas carol which, whilst widely sung, can really only be sung without hypocrisy by Christians. For it can only be truly sung by those who have been saved by the grace of God in Christ. It is as follows:

> Not in that poor lowly stable,
> With the oxen standing by,
> We shall see Him, but in heaven,
> Set at God's right hand on high;
> When like stars His children crowned
> All in white shall wait around.[4]

Reflect on these points

1. *Think of it: the eternal Son of God—the One through whom God made all things, the One who is dependent on nobody—lay in a manger as a helpless baby, completely dependent on others for support.*

2. *The Messiah had arrived. The angels of heaven were celebrating . . . but earth seemed indifferent. There was no great reception for the Saviour. He was crowded out. Folk went on their earth-bound course as normal. Things do not seem any different today.*

3. *If your faith is in the Christ of Bethlehem who became the Christ of Calvary, you have been embraced in God's*

gracious redemption. One day you will see Christ face to face and rejoice evermore that He was born for you at Bethlehem and died for you at Calvary to pay the price for your sins.

Light in the
darkness

One of the saddest days of my life was the day of my father's funeral. It was a dark, drizzly and murky winter's day. The weather outside seemed to mirror our mood inside. We had a service in church, giving thanks for my dad's life, and then went to the cemetery to bury him. Amazingly, though, at the exact moment when I helped lower his coffin into the ground, the clouds parted and the sun peeped out for a few moments. I took this as a little token of God's love. The funeral—like all funerals—was highly organized and arranged. But we could not have arranged for the clouds to part and the sun to shine briefly at the exact moment it did, completely contrary to the weather forecast of that day.

Spiritual darkness

Sadly, when sin came into the world, the whole world, via our first ancestors, was plunged into spiritual darkness—ignorance of God, rebellion against God, and a lack of fellowship and harmony between us and God our Maker. Sin brought a dark rift between creature and Creator. At the first Christmas, however, it was as though Almighty God parted the clouds, shone His light through and revealed His love and grace to fallen sinners. Of Isaiah's many messianic prophecies, in Isaiah 9:2, 6 we read,

> The people who walked in darkness
>   have seen a great light;
> those who dwelt in a land of deep darkness,
>   on them has light shined . . .

For to us a child is born,
    to us a son is given;
and the government will be upon his shoulder,
    and his name will be called
'Wonderful Counselor, Mighty God,
    Everlasting Father, Prince of Peace.'

This prophecy was most surely fulfilled in Christ at Christmas, for He was and is both the Child born and the Son given.

Likewise, the prophet Malachi foretold in Malachi 4:2 that 'the sun of righteousness shall rise, with healing in its wings'. Again, in Christ the prophecy was fulfilled. In his introduction to his Gospel, John explained, 'The true light that enlightens every man was coming into the world' (John 1:9). In the Christ who was born in Bethlehem, that 'true light' most surely came.

The Light of the world is Jesus

One of the many stupendous claims Jesus made is found in John 8:12, where He asserted, 'I am the light of the world; he who follows me will not walk in darkness, but will have the light of life.' Similarly, in John 12:46 He made the promise, 'I have come as light into the world, that whoever believes in me may not remain in darkness.' But what did Jesus mean here?

In the physical realm, it is light which dispels darkness and gloom. Likewise, in the spiritual realm it is Jesus who dispels our spiritual darkness. How? He does so in both His person and in His passion.

The person of Christ

It is Jesus who dispels our ignorance of God, because He is God in the flesh—God in a body; God in human form. Christmas is all about 'the incarnation'—that is, God becoming man in the Lord Jesus Christ. Jesus is 'Our God contracted to a span, incomprehensibly made man.'[1] In Christ, the incomprehensible became comprehensible. Paul could say of Him, 'For in him the whole fulness of deity dwells bodily' (Col. 2:9). And Jesus said of Himself, 'He who has seen me has seen the Father' (John 14:9); 'He who believes in me, believes not in me but in him who sent me' (John 12:44); and even 'he who sees me sees him who sent me' (John 12:45).

The passion of Christ

Most importantly, Jesus dispels the spiritual darkness which we are in by nature by His death on the cross—His passion. Salvation entails coming to the light of Christ and knowing reconciliation to God through the death of Christ for our sins. Christians are children of light because they belong to Jesus. Ephesians 5:8 says, 'For once you were darkness, but now you are light in the Lord.'

On the cross of Calvary, thirty-three years after His birth, Jesus endured the most terrible physical and spiritual darkness on behalf of His people. This was because our sins were put to His account. They were imputed to Him so that He could pay their penalty. Christ's birth at Bethlehem was solely with the cross of Calvary in mind. On the cross He suffered the wrath of God so that when we believe in Him we are saved from that wrath. On the cross He was momentarily separated from God the Father so that when we believe in Him we are reconciled to God the Father for time and eternity—transferred from the dominion of darkness into the kingdom of His everlasting light.

The message of Christmas is thus the message that this dark world desperately needs. It is a message of light and joy concerning 'a Savior, who is Christ the Lord' (Luke 2:11). No less than the Light of the world was born in that dark and dingy animal shelter at Bethlehem—and He invites us to come to that Light today!

> O little town of Bethlehem,
> How still we see thee lie;
> Above thy deep and dreamless sleep
> The silent stars go by:
> Yet in thy dark streets shineth
> The everlasting Light;
> The hopes and fears of all the years
> Are met in thee tonight.[2]

Reflect on these points

1. *Since its entrance into the world, sin has brought a dark rift between creature and Creator. At the first Christmas, however, it was as though Almighty God parted the clouds, shone His light through and revealed His love and grace to fallen sinners.*

2. *Jesus dispels our ignorance of God, because He is God in*

the flesh. In Christ, the incomprehensible became comprehensible.

3. *Christians are children of light because they belong to Jesus. They have been transferred from the dominion of darkness into the kingdom of His everlasting light.*

Christmas
jumpers

In recent years, the practice of having a designated 'Christmas jumper day' in the run-up to Christmas seems to have really taken off. We have such a day where I work. To take part, you have to contribute £1 to charity. Then you can wear your slightly garish Christmas jumper. Mine is green and red, and has the slogan 'Merry Christmas' across the front. When I wore it into work last year, I had company: the bus driver was also wearing a Christmas jumper. Personally, I don't think it's a bad idea. It puts a smile on faces on a dark December day.

The clothes of the infant Christ

When the Christ who lies behind Christmas was born in an animal shelter in Bethlehem, Scripture tells us that Mary His mother 'wrapped him in swaddling cloths' (Luke 2:7). This was no garish Christmas jumper, but the custom of the day in the Middle East. When a baby was born, he or she was rubbed with salt and oil, and then wrapped in long bands of cloth, somewhat like bandages. This gave the baby's limbs strength and protection. It also prevented the baby from scratching him- or herself, and it was believed to help babies sleep better.

So ponder the reality of this: the very Son of God was found as 'a babe wrapped in swaddling cloths [that is, baby bandages] and lying in a manger [that is, a trough for feeding animals]' (Luke 2:12). Here is a wonder of wonders! Here is a divine humiliation—coming down from a high rank to a low one; and Christ did this for us, in obedience to the divine plan. The Westminster Shorter Catechism distinguishes between Christ's states of humiliation and exaltation. Of the former it says: 'Christ's humiliation consisted in His being born, and that in a low condition, made under the law, undergoing the miseries of this life, the wrath of God, and the cursed death of the cross; in being buried, and continuing under the power of death for a time' (Question 27).

Put poetically, we may say:

> See! In yonder manger low,
> Born for us on earth below,
> See! The Lamb of God appears,
> Promised from eternal years.
>
> Lo! Within a manger lies
> He who built the starry skies,
> He who, throned in height sublime,
> Sits amid the cherubim.
>
> Sacred Infant, all Divine,
> What a tender love was Thine,
> Thus to come from highest bliss
> Down to such a world as this![1]

Christmas wrapping

We could consider Christ's swaddling clothes as the first Christmas wrapping on the first Christmas present. And what an unsurpassed and unsurpassable present! The Christ of Christmas is the Christ of the gospel. And Christ is the gospel and the gospel is Christ. 'God so loved the world that he gave his only Son, that whoever believes in him should not perish but have eternal life' (John 3:16). 'The free gift of God is eternal life in Christ Jesus our Lord' (Rom. 6:23). 'Thanks be to God for his inexpressible gift!' (2 Cor. 9:15).

Wearing the right clothes

If everyone in your office or at your Christmas party is wearing a Christmas jumper but for some reason you are not, it is a little embarrassing. It looks as if you are not playing. The Lord Jesus once told a parable of a similar situation, but with an infinitely more serious intent. He said, 'The kingdom of heaven may be compared to a king who gave a marriage feast for his son' (Matt. 22:2). He continued, 'But when the king came in to look at the guests, he saw there a man who had no wedding garment; and he said to him, "Friend, how did you get in here without a wedding garment?" And he was speechless' (Matt. 22:11–12). Sadly, the man was ejected from the joyful celebrations and cast into the outer darkness.

In Bible times, a wedding garment was given to those attending a wedding feast. This made everyone equal, whatever their earthly standing or status. One man, though, did it his own way, to his detriment, and wore his own clothes. The Lord Jesus told the parable as a warning. It illustrates the fact that our own righteousness does not fit us for heaven. The only righteousness which suffices is the righteousness of Christ, freely bestowed on us—imputed to us—by divine grace. Jesus alone lived a sinless life. He then offered up His life as an atoning sacrifice for our sins, so that we might be clothed with His righteousness and made fit for the kingdom of heaven. According to the Bible, salvation means being properly clothed! It is being clothed with the perfect righteousness of Christ. 'Put on the Lord Jesus Christ' (Rom. 13:14).

> I will greatly rejoice in the LORD,
>   my soul shall exult in my God;
> for he has clothed me with the garments of salvation,
>   he has covered me with the robe of righteousness.
> (Isa. 61:10)

You might wear a Christmas jumper at Christmas-time. But when you have to stand before Almighty God, will you be clothed in the perfect righteousness of Christ?

> Jesus, Thy blood and righteousness
> My beauty are, my glorious dress;
> 'Midst flaming worlds, in these arrayed,
> With joy shall I lift up my head.
>
> This spotless robe the same appears,
> When ruined nature sinks in years;
> No age can change its glorious hue,
> The robe of Christ is ever new.[2]

Reflect on these points

1. *The very Son of God was found as a babe wrapped in baby bandages and lying in a trough for feeding animals. Here is a divine humiliation—and Christ did this for us, in obedience to the divine plan!*

2. *What an unsurpassed and unsurpassable present! The Christ of Christmas is the Christ of the gospel.*

3. *Our own righteousness does not fit us for heaven. The only righteousness which suffices is the righteousness of Christ. Salvation means being properly clothed—with the perfect righteousness of Christ.*

Some wonders
of Christmas

Did the one true, living God really become a man and visit our planet? Christians affirm that He did, for it is all recorded as a matter of fact in the Bible. The stupendous fact of God becoming man—the incarnation—takes us to the heart of Christmas and the true wonder of it all. In 1 Timothy 3:16 we read, 'Great indeed, we confess, is the mystery of our religion: [God] was manifested in the flesh . . . ' The Nicene Creed states that the Lord Jesus Christ 'for us men and for our salvation came down from heaven, and was incarnate by the Holy Ghost of the Virgin Mary, and was made man'.

Read the following points slowly, and let some of the wonders of Christmas sink in.

- At Christmas, the Son of God became a Son of Man, that the sons of men might become the sons of God. The Bible says that 'by nature' we are 'children of wrath' (Eph. 2:3), that is, not the children of God. We are sinners, and sin is an affront to a holy God. Our sin alienates us from Him. Yet through Christ we may be reconciled to God—adopted into His family and able to know and love Him as our Father for time and eternity. 'Adoption' is one of the many New Testament synonyms for Christian salvation. Through the Christ who was born at Bethlehem and who died at Calvary, we may be adopted into God's family for ever! There could be no higher privilege or status. 'Adoption is an act of God's free grace, whereby we are received into the number, and have a right to all the privileges of the sons of God' (Westminster Shorter Catechism, Question 34).

- At Christmas, Christ the Son of God became poor, so that we might become truly and eternally rich. 'For you know the grace of our Lord Jesus Christ, that though he was rich, yet for your sake he became poor, so that by his poverty you might become rich' (2 Cor. 8:9). In God's plan of salvation, Christ left the glories of the Father's house and became poor. He was born in an outhouse. He eventually had no permanent home, for He said, 'Foxes have holes, and birds of the air have nests; but the Son of man has nowhere to lay his head' (Luke 9:58). Christ eventually died on a wooden cross, and the only earthly possessions He had to bequeath were His clothes. Yet Christ's poverty has made the believer eternally rich with the riches of eternal salvation. It is through Christ's death on the cross that our sins are forgiven, we are made right with God and, as we have already mentioned, we are adopted into His family. Having been adopted into God's family through Christ's atoning work, we are princes and princesses! We are the children of the King—'and if children, then heirs, heirs of God and fellow heirs with Christ' (Rom. 8:17). Through Christ we will inherit the kingdom of heaven! In Christ, then, we are rich indeed.

- At Christmas, Christ took on Himself our weakness in order to strengthen us by His power. It is incredible to think that the Infinite became an infant, and the One whose arms uphold the universe was Himself held in the arms of His earthly mother. But it was so. He came from heaven and was born as a helpless baby, as we all once were. Eventually, 'he was crucified in weakness' (2 Cor. 13:4). Yet it is through Christ's weakness that we are made strong in the grace of God, for the gospel of Christ is 'the power of God for salvation to every one who has faith' (Rom. 1:16). Christ is, says Paul, 'the power of God and the wisdom of God. For the foolishness of God is wiser than men, and the weakness of God is stronger than men' (1 Cor. 1:24–25).

• At Christmas, the immortal God took on Himself our mortality so that by His grace we, the mortal ones, could know His immortality. The immortal God cannot die. Yet Romans 6:23 tells us, 'The wages of sin is death.' Hence, the reason why God in Christ became man was so that He could die and, in doing so, pay the wages of our sin and bestow on us the gift of eternal life. The whole of Romans 6:23 reads, 'For the wages of sin is death, but the free gift of God is eternal life in Christ Jesus our Lord.' If we belong to Jesus, God has bestowed on us eternal life. And if we belong to Jesus, God will one day bestow on us immortality. For 'God raised the Lord and will also raise us up by his power' (1 Cor. 6:14).

• At Christmas, God descended to earth, that we might

go at last to heaven. It was 'for us and for our salvation' that 'He came down from heaven' (Nicene Creed). Heaven is the dwelling place of God. It is a place of light and joy. Our true joy is to know fellowship with God. Through Christ and all He has accomplished, we may realize our true joy and chief end. Through Him our sins are wiped off the record. Through Him we are reconciled to God. Through Him we become the children of God. Through Him our sins are washed away and we are thus made fit for heaven—for the nearer presence of God. One day, if we belong to Jesus, by His grace we shall be there!

Ponder these wonders of Christmas: that the Son of God became a Son of Man that the sons of men might become the sons of God; Jesus became poor so that we might know the riches of God's grace; Christ took on Himself our weakness so that we might be strengthened with His salvation; He took on Himself our human mortality so that we might be blessed with His divine immortality; and He came to earth so that we on earth, through His atoning work and accomplished salvation, might one day ascend to heaven, eternally saved by His precious blood. Praise His name! Christmas is truly a wonder-ful time!

Reflect on these points

1. *Our sin alienates us from God. Yet through Christ we may be reconciled to God—adopted into His family and*

able to know and love Him as our Father for time and eternity.

2. *At the first Christmas, the Infinite became an infant, and the One whose arms uphold the universe was Himself held in the arms of His earthly mother.*

3. *Our true joy is to know fellowship with God. Through Christ our sins are washed away and we are thus made fit for heaven. One day, if we belong to Jesus, by His grace we shall be there!*

The first ever Christmas carol

'O Little Town of Bethlehem', 'Hark! The Herald Angels Sing', 'Once in Royal David's City', 'O Come, All Ye Faithful' . . . We all have our favourite Christmas carols. Christmas carols are part of our Christian heritage. They capture the story and message of Christmas in verse. They also give articulation to Christian praise. For example, 'O come, let us adore Him, Christ the Lord.'

Did you know that the first ever Christmas carol was uttered by angelic beings and not human beings? Luke 2:13–14 tells of this first Christmas carol. It was uttered on the night of the first ever Christmas. In the fields surrounding Bethlehem, Luke tells us of 'a great company of the heavenly host [which] appeared with the angel, praising God and saying, "Glory to God in the highest heaven, and on earth peace to those on whom his favour rests"' (NIV). Let us analyse this Christmas carol a little more closely.

Christmas praise

We note that this first ever Christmas carol begins by saying 'Glory to God in the highest.' How different this is from some of today's messages, which seem to say words to the effect of 'Glory to man in the lowest.' Glory to God! Almighty God is the most blessed, glorious and greatest of all beings. He is incomparable; He is in a category all of His own. The goal of the universe is His great glory. Our chief end, according to the Westminster Shorter Catechism, is 'to glorify God, and to enjoy Him for ever' (Question 1). We may admire some of our fellow human beings for the abilities they have, but Almighty

God alone is to be worshipped and praised, for He alone is worthy of our worship and praise.

The multitude of angels had reason to glorify God. They did so because He had kept His promise and sent into the world 'a Savior, who is Christ the Lord' (Luke 2:11). As far back as Genesis 3:15, at the dawn of world history, God had promised that One would be born who would crush the head of Satan. He would overcome sin and death. He would undo the ravages of the Fall and restore sinners to harmony and fellowship with God our Maker. In the Lord Jesus Christ God fulfilled His promise. Jesus, the One born at Bethlehem, is the 'Savior, who is Christ the Lord'. Angels have no need of a Saviour. We do, because we are sinners by nature and practice. The gospel is that 'Christ Jesus came into the world to save sinners' (1 Tim. 1:15). And He did so by being born at Bethlehem and eventually offering up His sinless life on Calvary's cross as an atoning sacrifice for the sins of others.

Peace on earth?

'Glory to God in the highest heaven, and on earth peace . .' We live, of course, in a warring world, which is not at peace. Sadly, workplaces, families and nations all experience disharmony and conflict. Jesus, however, came to give us personal peace— peace with God. He came from heaven on a peace mission. By nature, we are at war with God. Our sin puts us under the wrath of God. God is angry at sinners. However, by paying the penalty on Calvary's cross for the sins of all who believe, Jesus has appeased the wrath of God for all who believe. He has procured our peace with God. Colossians 1:20 tells of His 'making peace by the blood of his cross'. Romans 5:1 affirms, 'Therefore, since we are justified by faith, we have peace with God through our Lord Jesus Christ.'

> Peace, perfect peace, in this dark world of sin?
> The blood of Jesus whispers peace within.[1]

So Jesus bestows on us personal peace. Scripture also teaches that Jesus will yet bring in universal peace, at the end of the age, when He comes again in power and great glory, and puts all His enemies under His feet.

Finally, we note that the first ever Christmas carol draws our attention to one of the fundamentals of the Christian faith:

The grace of God

'Glory to God in the highest heaven, and on earth peace to those on whom *His favour* rests.' The Lord Jesus Christ is the unsurpassed and unsurpassable expression and evidence of God's goodwill and favour to humanity, the ultimate expression of His grace—that is, of His undeserved kindness and unmerited favour to undeserving, indeed, ill-deserving, sinners. The message of Christmas is the message of the angels, which is the message of the Bible, which is the message of the gospel: that 'God so loved the world that he gave his only Son, that whoever believes in him should not perish but have eternal life' (John 3:16). 'When the goodness and loving kindness of God our Savior appeared, he saved us, not because of deeds done by us in righteousness, but in virtue of his own mercy' (Titus 3:4–5).

Salvation, according to the Bible, is solely due to the goodwill of God—His grace; His unmerited favour seen in His sending of His own Son to be the Saviour of all who put their trust in Him.

So there is the first ever Christmas carol. In that carol, the angels uttered their praise to God for what He had done, saying, 'Glory to God in the highest heaven, and on earth peace to those on whom His favour rests.' If we belong to Jesus, we have just cause to echo their praise. The hymnwriter put this into verse:

> All glory be to God on high
> And to the earth be peace;
> Goodwill, henceforth, from heaven to men
> Begin and never cease.[2]

Reflect on these points

1. *Almighty God is the most blessed, glorious and greatest of all beings. He is incomparable; He is in a category all of His own. He alone is to be worshipped and praised, for He alone is worthy of our worship and praise.*

2. *By nature, we are at war with God. Our sin puts us under the wrath of God. However, by paying the penalty on Calvary's cross for the sins of all who believe, Jesus has procured our peace with God.*

3. *Salvation is solely due to the goodwill of God—His grace;*

His unmerited favour seen in His sending of His own Son to be the Saviour of all who put their trust in Him.

Taking on
new things

Underneath the surface jollity, Christmas can be a sad time for some. At Christmastime we can be particularly aware of loved ones who are no longer with us. This is the case in my family, where my late father no longer joins us around the Christmas dinner table.

Losing a loved one, though, can sometimes be accompanied by small compensations. Since my father's death, my mother has been released from the twenty-four-hour care he needed, and is now able to take on activities she was prevented from doing when my father was alive. She is now more involved with her church and has also joined a choir and a reading group. She is also now free to travel.

Did you know that the Lord Jesus—He whose birth lies at the centre of Christmas—at certain moments in time took on matters which He had never before taken on? In eternity past, Jesus, as the second person of the divine Trinity, lived in the glory of heaven, in the ineffable fellowship which exists in the Trinity of God the Father, Son and Holy Spirit. On earth, He could speak to His Father of 'the glory which I had with thee before the world was made' (John 17:5). Yet Scripture reveals that at crucial moments in the divine plan of salvation, Jesus, the eternal Son of God, took upon Himself our human flesh and our human sin. Technically, these moments are known as the divine incarnation and the divine imputation.

The divine incarnation

In Jesus, God became man, taking upon Himself our human flesh. In Jesus, God actually shared our humanity. John wrote, 'The Word became flesh and dwelt among us, full of grace and truth' (John 1:14), and Paul explained that 'in Him [Christ] the whole fulness of deity dwells *bodily*' (Col. 2:9). It is the incarnation—God's real, actual, historical and historic 'enfleshment'—which takes us to the heart of Christmas: 'Christ, the Son of God, became man, by taking to Himself a true body, and a reasonable soul, being conceived by the power of the Holy Ghost, in the womb of the Virgin Mary, and born of her, yet without sin' (Westminster Shorter Catechism, Question 22).

The real humanity of Jesus reminds us that we have a God who really does understand our human lot from 'the inside'. He can never be accused of being far removed from our daily struggles in this fallen world. 'Jesus wept' (John 11:35), and He slept (Mark 4:38). He experienced fatigue (John 4:6), hunger (Mark 11:12) and thirst (John 19:28). Jesus also experienced mental turmoil (Mark 14:33) and received the barbs of those who sought to inflict psychological damage on Him (Matt. 27:39). Christians thus hold to the full humanity of Christ as much as they do to His absolute deity, for Scripture teaches both. His real humanity tells us that 'we have not a high priest who is unable to sympathize with our weaknesses, but one who in every respect has been tempted as we are, yet without sin' (Heb. 4:15).

But why did the Lord Jesus take on Himself our humanity? The answer of the Bible is: so that He could die. His incarnation was with a view to His immolation. Unusually, His birth was with a view to His death. Scripture teaches that Jesus' birth was a case of His taking on Himself our human flesh. But His death was a case of His taking on Himself our human sin.

The divine imputation

In words of infinite profundity, 2 Corinthians 5:21 states, 'For our sake he made him to be sin who knew no sin, so that in him we might become the righteousness of God.' Hebrews 9:28 similarly tells of 'Christ having been offered once to bear the sins of many'.

The Christian gospel proclaims that the sins which prevent our fellowship with God and access to heaven may be fully and forever forgiven. But they may be forgiven only because Christ took them and their consequences on Himself when He died on the cross. Our sins may be forgiven because Christ bore them. When we speak of Christ 'bearing' our sins, we mean that He paid the price for them; He paid the penalty for them; He endured the punishment which we should have borne for them. He became the sinner's substitute. Divine 'imputation' is the word which encapsulates this. Our sins, in the mercy of God, were 'put to Christ's account'. He 'paid the bill' so that we might be exonerated. On the cross of Calvary, He endured the wrath of God on our sins to save everyone who believes in Him from the wrath of God on their sins:

> All Thy sins were laid upon Him,
> Jesus bore them on the tree;

> God, who knew them, laid them on Him,
> And, believing, thou art free.[1]

So at two key points in the story of redemption, God, in Christ, took upon Himself our human flesh and also our human sin. The two may be distinguished, but they cannot be separated, as the former was with a view to the latter. Christ was born to save us. 'You shall call his name Jesus, for he will save his people from their sins' (Matt. 1:21). Salvation was actually procured, not by Christ's birth, but by His death, in the very last hours of His earthly life, when He died as an atoning sacrifice for sinners. Christ's taking on Himself our humanity was with the sole purpose of taking on Himself our sin. Christmas Day was with a view to Good Friday, for Christ's cradle was with a view to His cross, when 'He himself bore our sins in his body on the tree' (1 Peter 2:24).

> Jesus, my Saviour, to Bethlehem came,
> Born in a manger to sorrow and shame;
> Oh, it was wonderful—blest be His name!
> Seeking for me, for me!
>
> Jesus, my Saviour, on Calvary's tree,
> Paid the great debt and my soul He set free;
> Oh, it was wonderful—how could it be?
> Dying for me, for me![2]

Reflect on these points

1. The incarnation, the real humanity of Jesus, reminds us that we have a God who really does understand our human lot from 'the inside'. He can never be accused of being far removed from our daily struggles in this fallen world.

2. *Why did the Lord Jesus take on Himself our humanity? The answer of the Bible is: so that He could die. His incarnation was with a view to His immolation. His birth was with a view to His death. Christmas Day was with a view to Good Friday.*

3. *The sins which prevent our fellowship with God and access to heaven may be fully and forever forgiven. But they may be forgiven only because Christ took them and their consequences on Himself when He died on the cross.*

Santa or the Saviour?
Claus or Christ?
Compare and contrast

At this time of year, we cannot avoid encountering a jolly, rosy-cheeked, white-bearded gentleman in a red and white suit. He seems to be everywhere—on cards, in shops, in songs and in films. His name is Santa Claus, a.k.a. Father Christmas. As a young boy, like many I was very taken up with old Santa, and pushed any doubts and puzzles about him to the back of my mind. It did, though, come as something of a shock to find out, when I was about nine years old, that Santa was not actually real, and the presents he apparently brought came from another source: my mum and dad. I can remember the feeling of disappointment and of 'being had' to this day.

For the Christian, it is the Lord Jesus Christ who is the centre and focal point of Christmas, not Santa. And a comparison of the two is very revealing.

Reality, not mythology

First of all, Santa, with his supposed ability to fly through the sky on a sleigh, not to mention navigating all the blocked-up chimneys in town, is not actually real. He is make-believe. We are told that his red and white suit is a relatively recent invention; it was used first as an advertising ploy for a well-known soft drink.

The Lord Jesus Christ, however, is a historical figure, not a mythological one. He really existed, and He really exists. For example, 2 Peter 1:16 reads, 'For we did not follow cleverly devised myths when we made known to you the power and coming of our Lord Jesus Christ, but we were eyewitnesses of his majesty.' And all of the Gospel accounts have a 'ring of truth' about them. Luke's Gospel, for instance, describes the ministry of Jesus within the Roman Empire of the first century—specifically, 'in the fifteenth year of the reign of Tiberius Caesar, Pontius Pilate being governor of Judea, and Herod being tetrarch of Galilee' (Luke 3:1). Earlier, Luke had described the birth of Jesus as coinciding with the time when 'a decree went out from Caesar Augustus that all the world should be enrolled. This was the first enrollment, when Quirinius was governor of Syria' (Luke 2:1–2).

Yes, historical reality characterizes the Lord Jesus Christ. He is no invention; He is a historical figure who has divided history into BC and AD. We are now living in the twenty-first century AD—twenty-one hundred years after the birth of Christ at Bethlehem.

Temporary happiness or lasting joy?

Whilst Santa brings a degree of jollity and temporary cheer to the cold winter days, he brings no lasting joy. He is a bit irrelevant in the weeks after Christmas, and certainly in July. What a contrast with the Saviour and the blessing He brings!

> Fading is the worldling's pleasure,
> All his boasted pomp and show;
> Solid joys and lasting treasure
> None but Zion's children know.[1]

The original Christmas message concerns 'good news of a great joy . . . for to you is born this day in the city of David a Savior, who is Christ the Lord' (Luke 2:10–11). In John 15:11

Jesus says, 'These things I have spoken to you, that my joy may be in you, and that your joy may be full.' Christians alone know fullness of joy: a joy in the Lord, the joy of eternal salvation, the joy of being reconciled for ever to God our Maker through the Lord Jesus Christ and His atoning death.

Merited or unmerited favour?

Santa comes, we are told, to reward the good. Here we have a clash with the Bible, for the Bible teaches that if Santa came only to reward the good, he would not be able to come at all. Jesus said, 'No one is good but God alone' (Mark 10:18); Romans 3:12 states, 'No one does good, not even one'; and Ecclesiastes 7:20 says, 'Surely there is not a righteous man on earth who does good and never sins.'

In complete contrast to Santa, Jesus said, 'I came not to call the righteous, but sinners' (Mark 2:17). The Christian gospel in a nutshell is that 'Christ Jesus came into the world to save sinners' (1 Tim. 1:15). The blessing of salvation comes to those who confess that, by rights, they deserve punishment, not a reward; to those who, confessing their sin and guilt, cast themselves on Christ for mercy, for He alone is the Saviour of sinners:

> Nothing in my hand I bring,
> Simply to the cross I cling;
> Naked, come to Thee for dress;
> Helpless, look to Thee for grace;

Foul, I to the fountain fly;

Wash me, Saviour, or I die.[2]

A finished or unfinished work?

Legend has it that Santa comes every year on the night of 24 December/morning of 25 December. His work is thus never finished. We can expect him next year as well as this. This contrasts drastically with the work of Christ. Jesus came into the world to save sinners, and on Calvary's cross He actually procured their eternal salvation, once and for all, fully and for ever: 'He has appeared once for all at the end of the age to put away sin by the sacrifice of himself' (Heb. 9:26). 'When Christ had offered for all time a single sacrifice for sins, he sat down at the right hand of God' (Heb. 10:12). It is the 'finished work of Christ' which distinguishes the Christian faith and brings to the believing heart much assurance, reassurance and true hope.

Agreeable presents or the greatest Gift?

Finally, we note that Santa comes with gifts. Experience recalls that these are often very nice gifts, enjoyable and useful for a season. But at the heart of Christmas lies a Gift to dwarf all gifts: a priceless Gift beyond compare. God gave His own Son to be our Saviour. Our greatest need is for a Saviour, and in Christ alone we find the Saviour for our greatest need. Giving certainly lies at the centre of Christmas, but the giving in question is a divine, not a human, one: 'God so loved the world that he *gave* his only Son, that whoever believes in him should not perish but have eternal life' (John 3:16). 'The *free gift* of God is eternal life in Christ Jesus our Lord' (Rom. 6:23). 'Thanks be to God for his inexpressible *gift!*' (2 Cor. 9:15).

There, then, are some of the contrasts between the Saviour and Santa, Christ and Claus. I do not wish to enter into the controversial area of arguments for and against believing in Father Christmas, and whether he is harmful to children's spiritual growth or not. Sincere Christians are in disagreement here. I will, however, state that no one and nothing is to come between a Christian and their Saviour. Jesus is the reason for the season. He is the centrepiece of Christmas. He is the centrepiece of the Christian's life and joy—and He will be the focus and joy of the Christian throughout life, in death and for all eternity. Nothing can take the place of the Lord Jesus Christ—and knowing Him and His salvation, we will not want anyone or anything to usurp His place.

> Turn your eyes upon Jesus,
> Look full in His wonderful face,
> And the things of earth will grow strangely dim,
> In the light of His glory and grace.[3]

Reflect on these points

1. *Santa brings a degree of jollity and temporary cheer to the cold winter days, but he brings no lasting joy. He is irrelevant after Christmas. What a contrast with the Saviour and the blessing He brings!*

2. *Santa comes to reward the good. In complete contrast,*

Jesus said, 'I came not to call the righteous, but sinners' (Mark 2:17).

3. *Santa's work is never finished. We can expect him next year as well as this. But Jesus' work was to come into the world to save sinners, and on Calvary's cross He actually procured their eternal salvation, once and for all, fully and for ever.*

Santa or the Saviour?

The Twelve Days of Christmas

I am sure you have heard the well-known Christmas song entitled 'The Twelve Days of Christmas'. The song always seems to be heard during the Christmas season. I confess that I never used to give it much thought, as it comes over as nothing more than a frivolous ditty. I revised my opinion last Christmas, however, when I learned that 'The Twelve Days of Christmas' is actually Christian in origin. It was written during a time of religious persecution, when the faith was driven somewhat underground. Each line of the song contains a hidden Christian meaning, known only to Christians. This enabled the song to be sung in public without fear of arrest, for a non-Christian would know only its surface meaning. Let us delve a little deeper into this seemingly light-hearted song.

On the first day of Christmas my true love gave to me a partridge in a pear tree. 'My true love' here represents God the Father, the partridge represents His Son, the Lord Jesus Christ, and the 'pear tree' represents the cross of Calvary. A mother partridge, we are told, feigns injury to deter predators from harming her nestlings. And of course, in His great love, God the Father sent His Son into the world to be the Saviour of sinners, delivering them from eternal harm by dying in their place. In 1 John 4:10 we read, 'In this is love, not that we loved God but that he loved us and sent his Son to be the expiation for our sins.'

On the second day of Christmas my true love gave to me two turtle doves. These two turtle doves represent the Old and New Testaments which constitute the Bible. The Old and New

Testaments are the two lips by which God speaks to us. They are infallible and inerrant. They are inspired by God's Holy Spirit and reveal the Creator's secret of a happy life, a happy death and a happy eternity.

On the third day of Christmas my true love gave to me three French hens. These represent the three theological virtues of 'faith, hope and love' (1 Cor. 13:13). Faith means trusting in and relying on God. Hope is a confident assurance and expectation that God will be true to His promises. Love for God and love for our fellow believers is a virtue enjoined frequently in the New Testament.

On the fourth day of Christmas my true love gave to me four calling birds. The four calling birds here represent the four Gospels—Matthew, Mark, Luke and John. The Bible gives us four written portraits of the one Christ. Matthew portrays Him as the King of the Jews—the long-awaited Messiah. Mark portrays Him as the Servant of the Lord. Luke portrays Him as the Saviour of sinners. John portrays Him as the eternal Son of God who became man. All four Gospels major disproportionately on the death of Christ at Calvary. It is by the death of Christ, not His life, that sinners are reconciled to God.

On the fifth day of Christmas my true love gave to me five gold rings. These five gold rings represent the first five books of the Bible, the Pentateuch: Genesis, Exodus, Leviticus, Numbers and Deuteronomy. The theme of these five books is creation, the Fall and redemption. They tell us of our origins.

They tell us how sin has spoiled the world. They tell us that the way back to God is by the blood sacrifice He has ordained: the blood sacrifices of the Old Testament all prefigured and foreshadowed the one sacrifice of Christ in the New Testament.

On the sixth day of Christmas my true love gave to me six geese a-laying. The six laying geese here represent the six days of creation as revealed in Genesis 1. The Bible teaches that Almighty God is the Creator and Sustainer of the universe. He spoke the world into existence in six days, and rested on the seventh. 'In the beginning God created the heavens and the earth' (Gen. 1:1).

On the seventh day of Christmas my true love gave to me seven swans a-swimming. These seven swimming swans represent the seven gifts of the Holy Spirit in Romans 12:6–7, namely prophecy, service, teaching, exhortation, giving, helping and acts of mercy. The risen Christ, by His Spirit, bestows these gifts on His church for her welfare and edification. Whilst no Christian has all the gifts of the Spirit, every Christian has at least one of the gifts by which they can be a blessing to the church, which is the body of Christ. Paul's exhortation to Timothy is an exhortation to every Christian: 'Do not neglect the gift you have' (1 Tim. 4:14).

On the eighth day of Christmas my true love gave to me eight maids a-milking. The eight milking maids are the eight 'Beatitudes' with which the Lord Jesus opened His famous 'Sermon on the Mount', the greatest sermon ever preached. The key to the Beatitudes is the first one: 'Blessed are the poor in spirit, for theirs is the kingdom of heaven' (Matt. 5:3). True blessedness is a result of realizing our spiritual poverty and need, and casting ourselves on God in Christ for mercy.

On the ninth day of Christmas my true love gave to me nine ladies dancing. These nine dancing ladies represent the ninefold 'fruit of the Spirit' enunciated in Galatians 5:22–23— 'love, joy, peace, patience, kindness, goodness, faithfulness, gentleness, self-control'. The Holy Spirit of Christ gradually transforms Christians into the likeness of Christ. The process is known as sanctification. Fruit can take time to ripen, but, by the grace of God, all who belong to Jesus will surely ripen more and more into His character.

On the tenth day of Christmas my true love gave to me ten lords a-leaping. The ten leaping lords represent the Ten Commandments, as delivered by God to Moses at Mount Sinai. The Ten Commandments are the Maker's instructions. They are a summary of the moral law. They reveal God's will, and they convict us of our sin and drive us to Christ for salvation. They also show us how to please God. If we love Him, and if we have been saved by His grace, we will endeavour to keep His commandments.

On the eleventh day of Christmas my true love gave to me eleven pipers piping. Jesus chose twelve disciples, corresponding to the twelve tribes of Israel. Of these twelve, only eleven were faithful. One, Judas Iscariot, betrayed Him.

On the twelfth day of Christmas my true love gave to me twelve drummers drumming. This final line of the song was intended to be a surreptitious reminder of the twelve lines of the Apostles' Creed. The Apostles' Creed is an early summary of the faith of the Bible—the trinitarian faith in God the Father, Son and Holy Spirit, 'the faith which was once for all delivered to the saints' (Jude 3). The Apostles' Creed is distinctly trinitarian as the Christian faith is distinctly trinitarian. A Christian is one who has been saved by God the Holy Trinity—'chosen and destined by God the Father and sanctified by the Spirit for obedience to Jesus Christ and for sprinkling with his blood' (1 Peter 1:2).

So while 'The Twelve Days of Christmas' comes over as a jolly song, and somewhat light-hearted, there is more to it than meets the eye. Once we know its hidden meaning, we will never sing or hear it in the same way again. Happy Christmas!

Reflect on these points

1. *The four Gospels major disproportionately on the death of Christ at Calvary. It is by the death of Christ, not His life, that sinners are reconciled to God.*

2. *True blessedness is a result of realizing our spiritual poverty and need, and casting ourselves on God in Christ for mercy.*

3. *The Holy Spirit of Christ gradually transforms Christians into the likeness of Christ. Fruit can take time to ripen, but, by the grace of God, all who belong to Jesus will surely ripen more and more into His character.*

'Good King Wenceslas looked out on the feast of Stephen...'

The good duke

S hould you ever visit Prague in the Czech Republic, you will be able to see a statue of no less a celebrity than 'Good King Wenceslas'. The statue stands, fittingly, in 'Wenceslas Square'. 'King Wenceslas' has become immortalized in the lilting Christmas carol sung about him, although, technically, the 'Feast of Stephen' referred to in the first verse refers to 26 December, not Christmas Day.

Wenceslas, contrary to the carol, was not a king but a duke. He was the Duke of Bohemia from AD 907 to 935. By all accounts he was a very godly and gracious man. Humanly speaking, this was due to his having been brought up in the Christian faith by Ludmila, his grandmother. Although I am somewhat sceptical about medieval history—I am never quite sure where history ends and legends begin—I have no reason to doubt what one Cosmas of Prague wrote about Wenceslas in 1119, some two hundred years after the latter's dukedom:

> But his deeds I think you know better than I
> could tell you . . . no one doubts that, rising every
> night from his noble bed, with bare feet and
> only one chamberlain, he went around to God's
> churches and gave alms generously to widows,
> orphans, those in prison and afflicted by every
> difficulty, so much so that he was considered, not
> a prince, but the father of all the wretched.[1]

Christian giving

The carol 'Good King Wenceslas' is set on a bitterly cold winter's day. Wenceslas looks out of his window and notices a poor peasant battling against both the cold and poverty. He takes pity on him and relieves him of his need by inviting him into the warmth of his palace and giving him a hearty meal. The song ends by telling all Christian men that 'Ye who now will bless the poor shall yourselves find blessing.' This ties in with the words of the Lord Jesus Himself, for He said that 'it is more blessed to give than to receive' (Acts 20:35).

Paradoxically, there is, as Wenceslas knew, a blessing gained in giving, especially when it relieves another's need. The book of Proverbs says,

> One man gives freely, yet grows all the richer;
>> another withholds what he should give, and only
>>> suffers want.
> A liberal man will be enriched,
>> and one who waters will himself be watered.
> (Prov. 11:24–25)

> He who is kind to the poor lends to the LORD,
>> and he will repay him for his deed.
> (Prov. 19:17)

The social need which Wenceslas relieved was a need for food, shelter and warmth. Needs today, though, can fit into a less tangible category. Many have a need for friendship, sympathy and a listening, understanding ear. We can give of ourselves, even if we cannot give of our finances. When we do so, we find, as Jesus said, that 'it is more blessed to give than to receive'.

A picture of the gospel

Thinking about the kindness of 'Good King Wenceslas'—a rich man of means who enriched a poor, needy man of no means—it occurred to me that we have here an illustration of the very gospel of God. The God of the universe owns everything. The God of the Bible, to quote the Westminster Confession, 'hath all life, glory, goodness, blessedness, in and of Himself; and is alone in and unto Himself all-sufficient, not standing in need of any creatures which He hath made, nor deriving any glory from them, but only manifesting His own glory in, by, unto and upon them'. Yet, according to the Bible, this God—amazing as it sounds—actually invites poor sinners into His banqueting house to feast with Him! Every Christian can testify: 'He brought me to the banqueting house, and his banner over me was love' (S. of S. 2:4). The Christian gospel—and the ultimate message of Christmas—is of God's grace to poor, bankrupt sinners. 'For you know the grace of our Lord Jesus Christ, that though he was rich, yet for your sake he became poor, so that by his poverty you might become rich' (2 Cor. 8:9).

By nature, we could not be more spiritually poor or needy. We are sinners, liable to God's wrath. We cannot buy our way out of our predicament. But, in amazing grace, God sent His Son from heaven to be born at Bethlehem and to die at Calvary, so that our sins might be forgiven and we might be reconciled to God our Maker for time and eternity. In Jesus we may fulfil our chief end of knowing, loving and enjoying God. He alone makes this possible.

No gospel like this feast

The Christian gospel, then, may be likened to a feast. It is a feast prepared and provided by God Himself for poor, needy sinners. And God, in Christ, by His Spirit, still invites sinners to partake of this glorious feast, even today. In Jesus and His promise of salvation, the provision of Isaiah 25:6 is ultimately realized. There we read, 'On this mountain the LORD of hosts will make for all peoples a feast of fat things, a feast of wine on the lees, of fat things full of marrow, of wine on the lees well refined.' The gospel is actually a gracious invitation from the King of the universe to come and dine—to come and partake of His provision in Jesus for our soul's eternal blessedness. In Matthew 22:2ff. we read: 'The kingdom of heaven may be compared to a king who gave a marriage feast for his son, and sent his servants to call those who were invited . . . '"I have made ready my dinner . . . come to the marriage feast."' Luke 14:17 is both an invitation and an exhortation: 'Come; for all is now ready.'

Salvation, then, according to the Bible, is as simple and yet as profound as feasting with God! 'O taste and see that the LORD is good! Happy is the man who takes refuge in him!' (Ps. 34:8).

No gospel like this feast
Spread for us, Lord, by Thee;
No prophets or evangelists
Preach the glad news more free.

This was the bitter price,
Ours is the free gift given;
This was the blood of sacrifice,
Ours is the wine of heaven.[2]

Reflect on these points

1. *Many today have a need for friendship, sympathy and a listening, understanding ear. We can give of ourselves, even if we cannot give of our finances. When we do so, we find, as Jesus said, that 'it is more blessed to give than to receive'.*

2. *The God of the universe owns everything. And we could not be more spiritually poor or needy. Yet, according to the Bible, this God—amazing as it sounds—actually invites us poor sinners into His banqueting house to feast with Him!*

3. *The gospel is a gracious invitation from the King of the universe to come and dine—to come and partake of His provision in Jesus for our soul's eternal blessedness.*

The place of the Saviour's birth

Some seven hundred years before Christ's birth, the prophet Micah was enabled by God to prophesy that the Messiah would be born in a specific place, namely 'Bethlehem Ephrathah' (Micah 5:2). In God's sovereign timing, the prophecy was fulfilled to the letter 'when Jesus was born in Bethlehem of Judea' (Matt. 2:1).

First mention

Bethlehem is first mentioned in the Bible way back in Genesis 35, during the time of the patriarch Jacob. There it was the location of the death of Rachel, Jacob's wife. Sadly, Rachel died as she gave birth to Benjamin. Genesis 35 also contains the first reference to a gravestone in the Bible, for 'Jacob set up a pillar upon her [that is, Rachel's] grave; it is the pillar of Rachel's tomb, which is there to this day' (Gen. 35:20). Rachel's tomb can indeed still be seen today on the outskirts of Bethlehem, six or so miles outside Jerusalem.

Whenever the 'little town of Bethlehem' is mentioned, Christians immediately think of the birth of Christ and its centrality in the divine plan of salvation. Bethlehem and the holy nativity are inextricably intertwined. With biblical hindsight, however, we also see that Rachel's giving birth to Benjamin in Bethlehem draws our attention to Christ and His work of redemption as well.

Scripture records that 'Rachel travailed, and she had hard labor' (Gen. 35:16). Her birth pains proved to be fatal. This being so, 'as her soul was departing (for she died), she called [her son's] name Ben-oni' (35:18). The name 'Ben-oni' means

'Son of my sorrow'. Here we glimpse the Christ who was to come, for it was written of Him that 'he was despised and rejected by men; *a man of sorrows*, and acquainted with grief' (Isa. 53:3). It was also prophesied of Him, using the prophetic past tense:

> Look and see
> if there is any *sorrow like my sorrow*
>   which was brought upon me,
> which the LORD inflicted
>   on the day of his fierce anger.
> (Lam. 1:12)

The sorrows of Christ reached their culmination when He died on the cross and was momentarily separated from the fellowship with His Father He had always enjoyed. When Christ died on the cross, He bore the sins of God's people and God's righteous anger on them. His suffering and sorrow cannot be described—yet the Christian is eternally grateful for them. His sorrow is the source of our eternal joy. His suffering wrought our salvation. He endured the wrath of God on our sins to save us from it. 'Since, therefore, we are now justified by his blood, much more shall we be saved by him from the wrath of God' (Rom. 5:9). Jesus therefore is the true 'Ben-oni', 'Son of my sorrow'.

Jacob, however, overruled his dying wife's wishes, for he 'called [the child's] name Benjamin' (Gen. 35:18). The name 'Benjamin' means 'Son of the right hand'. Scripture states, 'When Christ had offered for all time a single sacrifice for sins, he sat down at the right hand of God' (Heb. 10:12). The 'right hand of God' refers to the place of supreme honour, pre-eminence and power. God the Father's satisfaction with and endorsement of His Son's atoning death was seen in His raising Him from the dead, and enthroning Him at His right hand in heaven. The Saviour who was born in Bethlehem and who died at Calvary is currently seated at God's right hand. Jesus is thus the true Benjamin as well as the true Ben-oni.

What's in a name?

'Bethlehem' refers to a town. 'Ephrathah' refers to the district in which Bethlehem was situated. The name 'Bethlehem' means 'house of bread'. The name 'Ephrathah' means 'fruitful'. Bethlehem's soil was evidently fertile, as the grain fields portrayed in the book of Ruth reveal. Here again, though, with New Testament hindsight, we see Jesus. He said of Himself, 'I am the bread of life; he who comes to me shall not hunger, and he who believes in me shall never thirst' (John 6:35), as well as proclaiming, 'I am the vine, you are the branches. He who abides in me, and I in him, he it is that bears much fruit, for apart from me you can do nothing' (John 15:5).

Remarkably, 'Bethlehem Ephrathah' also draws our attention to the Lord's Supper—one of the two ordinances bequeathed to us by Christ so that we may continually remember His death and the eternal benefits accomplished by it.

The Lord's Supper

'Bethlehem Ephrathah': bread and fruit. Bread is the product of crushed grain; wine is the product of crushed grapes; and it is by the simple and perishable emblems of bread and wine that Christ would have His disciples in all eras ever remember Him—or, more particularly, remember His atoning death. Non-Christians may find it strange, but the stress of the Christian faith is not so much on the birth of Christ at Bethlehem as on the death of Christ at Calvary, for it was on the cross of Calvary that eternal salvation was actually procured. Hence Christ's ordaining the ordinance of the Lord's Supper, where the broken bread and poured-out wine draw the believer's focus to the cross of Christ, where Christ's sinless body was broken and His precious blood shed for the sinner's redemption. Bishop J. C. Ryle put it eloquently:

> The Lord Jesus Christ knew full well the unspeakable importance of His own death as the great corner-stone of Scriptural religion. He knew that His own satisfaction for sin as our Substitute—His suffering for sin, the Just for the unjust—His payment of our mighty debt in His own Person—His complete redemption of us by His blood—He knew that this was the very root of soul-saving and soul-satisfying Christianity. Without this He knew His incarnation, miracles, teaching, example and ascension could do no good to man; without this He knew there could be no justification, no reconciliation, no hope, no peace between God and man. Knowing all this, He took care that *His death*, at any rate, should never be forgotten.

He carefully appointed an ordinance, in which, by lively figures [bread and wine], His sacrifice on the cross should be kept in perpetual remembrance.[1]

Bethlehem. It predates Christ's birth in Scripture. When we dig deeper, though, it leads us to ponder the death of Christ, as well as His birth. And this is surely fitting as, in the Bible, all roads lead to Calvary, for redemption was accomplished not by Christ's birth but by His death. Jesus was born to die. It has been well said that unless the cross overshadows the cradle, we will miss the true meaning of Christmas.

Reflect on these points

1. *Jesus is the true 'Ben-oni', 'Son of my sorrow'. His suffering and sorrow cannot be described, yet they are the source of our eternal joy. His suffering wrought our salvation.*

2. *Jesus is also the true Benjamin, 'Son of the right hand'. The Saviour who was born in Bethlehem and who died at Calvary is currently seated at God's right hand.*

3. *The stress of the Christian faith is not so much on the birth of Christ at Bethlehem as on His death at Calvary. Hence, in the Lord's Supper, the broken bread and poured-out wine draw the believer's focus to the cross of Christ, where Christ's sinless body was broken and His precious blood shed for the sinner's redemption.*

The royal birth

How do you announce a royal birth? In the UK, when a new addition to the royal family is born, the tradition is to put up a framed notice on a ceremonial easel outside Buckingham Palace. This is left there for twenty-four hours, and the news soon spreads around the world.

Some of our celebrities are treated almost as if they were royalty. When they have a birth, they take to social media. Their followers lap up the news, and the tabloid papers follow suit.

Christ's birth at Bethlehem at the first Christmas was truly a royal birth, for He is described in the Bible as the 'King of kings and Lord of lords' (Rev. 19:16). And when He was born, the announcement was made by 'an angel of the Lord' (Luke 2:9) sent from heaven. The angel—the word 'angel' means 'messenger'—proclaimed to some frightened shepherds in the fields surrounding Bethlehem, 'to you is born this day in the city of David a Savior, who is Christ the Lord' (Luke 2:11). So the Royal Birth which occurred 'once in royal David's city' was announced first to some humble shepherds as they went about their night-time routine.

Why was this stupendous announcement made to shepherds, and anonymous ones at that? The Bible gives us no clues, yet we can apply a bit of sanctified speculation:

- It was fitting for Christ's birth to be announced first to shepherds as the Lord Jesus was to describe Himself as a shepherd. In John 10:11 He affirmed, 'I am the good shepherd. The good shepherd lays down his life for the sheep.' This claim reveals Jesus' love and care, and also alludes to His death in the place of sinners. The claim was also a tacit claim to deity, for the God of the Old Testament is described many times as a shepherd. Psalm 80:1, for instance, begins with the prayer to God: 'Give ear, O Shepherd of Israel, thou who leadest Joseph like a flock!' Jesus was claiming to be co-equal with God.

• It was fitting for Christ's birth to be announced first to shepherds as the shepherds' chief role was tending lambs. Lambs were integral to the religious economy of Israel in those days. They were sacrificed in the temple in Jerusalem. God had ordained sacrifice—one dying in the place of another—as the means of atoning for sin. It was the death of an unblemished lamb, and the application of its blood, which brought deliverance from the angel of judgement at the first Passover. God said, 'When I see the blood, I will pass over you' (Exod. 12:13). In John 1:29, at the outset of Jesus' public ministry, we read of John the Baptist pointing to Jesus and proclaiming, 'Behold, the Lamb of God, who takes away the sin of the world!' And Jesus was born to die— to be sacrificed. The purpose of His coming was His crucifixion. His birth was with a view to His death, and His death was an atoning sacrifice of eternal validity. His death brought an end to the necessity of any more sacrifice. All who put their faith in the atoning death of the Lamb of God are saved eternally.

• Lastly, there might just be a deeper reason why the Royal Birth of Christ was first announced to shepherds. Shepherds were outcasts of society in those days. They were, as the hymn says, 'lowly'. They were low down on the social scale, and considered ritually unclean. Such people are often more receptive to the grace of God than those who are higher up in society and satisfied with their lot, and even self-righteous. Jesus warned against 'some who trusted in themselves that they were righteous and despised others' (Luke 18:9). Paul wrote to some Christians based in Corinth, 'For consider your call, brethren; not many of you were wise according to worldly standards, not many were powerful, not many were of noble birth; but God chose what is foolish in the world to shame the wise, God chose what is weak in the world to shame the strong, God chose what is low and despised in the world, even things that are not, to bring to nothing things that are, so that no human being might boast in the presence of God. He is the source of your life in Christ Jesus' (1 Cor. 1:26–30). It is a case of 'Where meek souls will receive Him still, the dear Christ enters in.'[1] Before we will trust Christ as our Saviour, we have to realize that we are in desperate, dire and damnable need of a Saviour—and that takes honesty and humility.

So the Royal Birth of Christ was announced first of all by an angel from heaven to some humble shepherds. And, of course, that glorious announcement is still announced in the Word of God to you and me. The announcement was nothing less than the gospel—a Saviour for lost, condemned sinners. The Royal Birth and the Royal Gospel is still to be proclaimed: 'to you is born this day in the city of David a Savior, who is Christ the Lord' (Luke 2:11).

> To us a child of royal birth,
> Heir of the promises, is given;
> The Invisible appears on earth,
> The Son of man, the God of heaven.
>
> A Saviour born, in love supreme
> He comes our fallen souls to raise;
> He comes His people to redeem
> With all His plenitude of grace.
>
> The Christ by raptured seers foretold,
> Filled with the eternal Spirit's power,
> Prophet and Priest and King behold,
> And Lord of all the worlds adore.
>
> The Lord of hosts, the God most high,
> Who quits His throne on earth to live,
> With joy we welcome from the sky,
> With faith into our hearts receive.[2]

Reflect on these points

1. The Lord Jesus was to describe Himself as 'the good

*shepherd . . . [who] lays down his life for the sheep'.
This claim reveals Jesus' love and care, and also alludes
to His death in the place of sinners.*

2. *Christ's death brought an end to the necessity of any
more sacrifice. All who put their faith in the atoning
death of the Lamb of God are saved eternally.*

3. *Before we will trust Christ as our Saviour, we have to
realize that we are in desperate, dire and damnable need
of a Saviour—and that takes honesty and humility.*

Joseph: the unsung hero of Christmas?

Joseph, the legal guardian and earthly father of the Lord Jesus, is often overlooked in the Christmas story. Matthew's Gospel, however, relates the account of the birth of Christ more from Joseph's perspective than from Mary's. Matthew tells us: 'Now the birth of Jesus Christ took place in this way. When his mother Mary had been betrothed to Joseph, before they came together she was found to be with child of the Holy Spirit; and her husband Joseph, being a just man and unwilling to put her to shame, resolved to divorce her quietly' (Matt. 1:18–19).

From the above, if we could imagine an interview with Joseph, the conversation might surely have gone something like this:

Interviewer: Tell me about the birth of Jesus.

Joseph: I was engaged to Mary. The marriage was arranged, as our marriages always are. I was both delighted and excited. I was a fair bit older than Mary, but I was struck by her beauty. She also came across as being very devout and godly. She loved the Scriptures and was devoted to the Lord God of our fathers. I was looking forward to our wedding day and, in the will of the Lord, to subsequently living our lives together.

Interviewer: So life could not have been better, then?

Joseph: Not quite. I was stopped in my tracks. To my horror and devastation, I found out that Mary was expectant. This was nothing to do with me. I had not been near her, and would not be so until after Jesus was born. I thought the worst: Mary had surely been unfaithful. It could have been one of those feckless Roman soldiers . . . My marriage was over before it had begun! Divorce was my only option. The engagement was legally binding. Yet I still loved Mary. I didn't want to compound her shame and difficulty, so I sought to divorce her as quietly and painlessly as possible.

Interviewer: But you didn't.

Joseph: No, indeed. Angelic visitations are rare in our Scriptures, but I had one. An angel actually came to me! He addressed me personally and authoritatively. I had no doubt that this messenger was from the Lord God Himself. 'Joseph, son of David, do not fear to take Mary your wife, for that which is conceived in her is of the Holy Spirit' [Matt. 1:20]. My sorrow turned to ecstatic joy. I realized that of all the women in Israel, my future spouse had been chosen to give birth to the longed-for Messiah! God had fulfilled His promise spoken centuries ago by His prophet: 'Behold, a young woman [or 'virgin'] shall conceive and bear a son, and shall call His name Immanuel' [Isa. 7:14]. Far from being unfaithful or immoral, Mary was merely submitting to and being obedient to the will of God. It was this heavenly visitation which carried me through the days ahead. I could cope with the stigma and cruel gossip of our neighbours in Nazareth. I resolved to be the best support to Mary that I could be. I travelled with her all the way back to my home town in Bethlehem, to undertake my enrolment there, knowing that the God who had foreordained all this would protect us. Of course, it was while we were in

Bethlehem that Jesus was born—again in fulfilment of ancient prophecy. God always keeps His word, and God always accomplishes His will.

Interviewer: Did you have any difficulty in deciding what to call Mary's firstborn?

Joseph: No. We actually had no choice. The angel commanded me, 'You shall call his name Jesus, for he will save his people from their sins' [Matt. 1:21].

It is here that we stop our imaginary interview with Joseph. Scripture does not actually tell us much more about him. It is likely that he died before Jesus reached adulthood, as he doesn't feature in the Gospel accounts during Jesus' earthly ministry. Matthew, though, concludes his account of the nativity with the words 'he [Joseph] called his name Jesus' (Matt. 1:25).

We can say, though, that we now know more than Joseph did then. He knew that the name Jesus meant 'Saviour'. But he did not live to see the procurement of the salvation Jesus came to bring. Jesus wrought the sinner's salvation, not by His birth, but by His death—by His cross, not His cradle. Jesus was born to die. His birth at Bethlehem was with a view to His death at Calvary. On Calvary's cross, He offered His sinless life as an atoning sacrifice, 'that whoever believes in him should not perish but have eternal life' (John 3:16). He died in the place of sinners. He died to 'save his people from their sins' (Matt.

1:21). He died to save us from the wrath of God. He died to reconcile us to God.

We are all sinners. We are all thus liable to the wrath of God. We all have need of a Saviour. In the Christ who was conceived by the Holy Spirit, born at Bethlehem and died on the cross of Calvary, we meet the Saviour we so desperately need. This is the wonder of Christmas. 'You shall call his name Jesus, for he will save his people from their sins' (Matt. 1:21). It is wonderful, and it is exclusive, for the Bible says, 'There is salvation in no one else, for there is no other name under heaven given among men by which we must be saved' (Acts 4:12).

Reflect on these points

1. *We now know more than Joseph did then. He knew that the name Jesus meant 'Saviour', but he did not live to see the procurement of the salvation Jesus came to bring.*

2. *This is the wonder of Christmas: 'You shall call his name Jesus, for he will save his people from their sins' (Matt. 1:21).*

3. *The message of Christmas is exclusive, for the Bible says, 'There is salvation in no one else, for there is no other name under heaven given among men by which we must be saved' (Acts 4:12).*

Joseph: the unsung hero of Christmas?

The original
satnav

I am embarrassed to confess that my technological expertise doesn't stretch much beyond sharpening a pencil. My brothers, though, always seem to keep up with the latest technology and use it to their advantage. For example, my younger brother has a satnav in his car. What is a satnav? A satnav uses a combination of satellite and mapping software to determine a car's position and plan the best route to a chosen destination. Before he sets off, my brother programmes the satnav by keying in his destination; then, while he travels, the satnav shouts out commands: 'Turn right at the next junction.' 'Take the second turning at the next roundabout.' Eventually it will say, 'You have reached your destination.' Amazing! It would seem that the days of the humble map in the glove compartment are long gone!

The holy star of Christ

In Matthew 2 you can read of the original satnav. Some Magi—or wise men—from Persia were guided to the infant Christ in Jerusalem by following a special star. On arriving in Jerusalem they asked King Herod, 'Where is he who has been born king of the Jews? For we have seen his star in the East, and have come to worship him' (Matt. 2:2). Verse 9 continues, 'They went their way; and lo, the star which they had seen in the East went before them, till it came to rest over the place where the child was.'

Mysteriously, then, it was a star which guided these Gentile men to the King of the Jews—the infant Christ. The account reaches a climax in verse 11 when it relates how 'they fell down and worshiped him'—only God is to be worshipped, so they recognized Jesus as God in the flesh. 'Then, opening their treasures, they offered him gifts, gold and frankincense and myrrh.'

> As with gladness men of old
> Did the guiding star behold;
> As with joy they hailed its light,
> Leading onward, beaming bright;
> So, most gracious Lord, may we
> Evermore be led to Thee.
>
> As with joyful steps they sped
> To that lowly cradle-bed,
> There to bend the knee before
> Thee whom heaven and earth adore;
> So may we with willing feet
> Ever seek Thy mercy seat.[1]

Almighty God is free to use any means He sees fit to draw people to Christ. Yet we have to admit that a star is not His normal way of operation. The Magi, though, were astrologers, and God met them where they were, and revealed to them the special significance of the special star which appeared in the sky. It signified that the Messiah had been born. The wise men may also have known an ancient Scripture, perhaps bequeathed to them by the prophet Daniel who had been exiled in their land many years before their time. Numbers 24:17 reads, 'A star shall come forth out of Jacob, and a scepter shall rise out of Israel.' This Scripture was now most surely fulfilled, for the King of kings had been born of the Virgin Mary.

The Holy Spirit of Christ

We have said that it was a star which guided the wise men to Christ. It was, and it wasn't! Ultimately, it was Almighty God Himself who drew them to Him, for Jesus explained in John 6:44, 'No one can come to me unless the Father who sent me draws him.' And thank God that He still draws people to Christ, even today. He does so, not by a star, but by His Holy Spirit. It is the Holy Spirit of God who reveals to us our need of Christ and the Christ for our need. It is He who convicts us of our sin and lost plight. It is He who draws us to Christ. It is He who nurtures in us saving faith in Christ, enabling us to trust Him as our own personal Saviour, and receive the benefits of His atoning death at Calvary—the forgiveness of sins, peace with God and the sure hope of eternal life. The technical term for this is 'effectual calling'.

> Q: What is effectual calling?
>
> A: Effectual calling is the work of God's Spirit, whereby, convincing us of our sin and misery, enlightening our minds in the knowledge of Christ, and renewing our wills, He doth persuade and enable us to embrace Jesus Christ, freely offered to us in the gospel.
>
> (The Westminster Shorter Catechism, Question 31)

The divine satnav

So the Holy Spirit from heaven is the divine satnav. He guides us to heaven because He guides us to Christ, who is the only way to heaven. Jesus affirmed, 'I am the way, and the truth, and the life; no one comes to the Father, but by me' (John 14:6). Thank God for His Holy Spirit, and thank God for His effectual calling. The gospel of Christ is a matter of divine redemption—divinely accomplished and divinely applied.

> Blessed Jesus, every day
> Keep us in the narrow way;
> And when earthly things are past,
> Bring our ransomed souls at last.
> Where they need no star to guide,
> Where no clouds Thy glory hide.[2]

Reflect on these points

1. *Almighty God is free to use any means He sees fit to draw people to Christ. He still draws people to Christ, even today. He does so, not by a star, but by His Holy Spirit.*

2. *It is the Holy Spirit of God who reveals to us our need of Christ and the Christ for our need. It is He who convicts us of our sin and lost plight. It is He who draws us to Christ.*

3. *The Holy Spirit guides us to heaven because He guides us to Christ, who is the only way to heaven.*

A Christmas blessing

Christmas Eve 2011 saw my family and I attending a service of 'Nine Lessons and Carols' in Bath Abbey. The carefully chosen readings from the Bible tracing the grand story of redemption, along with the traditional Christmas carols which paraphrased the readings, proved to be a great joy and blessing. The service concluded with the following prayer which has lodged in my mind:

> May the joy of the angels, the eagerness of the
> shepherds, the perseverance of the wise men,
> the obedience of Joseph and Mary and the peace
> of the Christ-child be yours this Christmas;
> and the blessing of God Almighty, the Father,
> the Son and the Holy Spirit, be among you
> and remain with you always. Amen.

Unpacking this prayer, we note that it refers first of all to *the joy of the angels*. It was some angels from heaven who announced the Saviour's birth at the first Christmas. They described this as 'good news of a *great joy* which will come to all the people' (Luke 2:10). What exactly constitutes this good and joyful news, though? The next verse tells us specifically: 'for to you is born this day in the city of David a *Savior*, who is Christ the Lord' (Luke 2:11). The joy, then, is that there is a Saviour. Our greatest need is for a Saviour, as we are sinners, under the judgement of God. In the Christ who was born at Bethlehem we find the Saviour for our greatest need. 'Christ Jesus came into the world to *save* sinners' (1 Tim. 1:15). 'For God sent the Son into the world, not to condemn the world, but that the world might be *saved* through him' (John 3:17). True Christmas joy, therefore, and true Christian joy, is knowing Jesus as our own personal Saviour—being a beneficiary of His saving work, and receiving through Him the forgiveness of our sins and the consequent peace with God and sure hope of eternal life.

Secondly, the prayer refers to *the eagerness of the shepherds*. As soon as the shepherds in the fields surrounding Bethlehem heard the good news of the Saviour's birth, they moved. They said, 'Let us go over to Bethlehem and see this thing that has happened, which the Lord has made known to us.' They did not dawdle, but 'went with haste, and found Mary and Joseph, and the babe lying in a manger' (Luke 2:15–16). And, of course, there is an urgency about the message of salvation, for salvation is the most crucial matter of all. Our attitude towards Jesus actually determines where we will spend eternity. If God has truly called us to Christ in the gospel, we will eagerly embrace the grace He offers us there without delay. 'Behold, now is the acceptable time; behold, now is the day of salvation' (2 Cor. 6:2).

Thirdly, the prayer refers to *the perseverance of the wise men*. This takes us to Matthew 2. There we read of some Magi from the East—Persia—who made a long, arduous journey to Bethlehem to see the infant Christ. This being before the days of modern transport, their journey was no doubt difficult and uncomfortable, but their motivation enabled them to persevere. And their faith, hope and love were abundantly rewarded, for at their journey's end their eyes eventually beheld the longed-for Messiah. 'Going into the house they saw the child with Mary his mother, and they fell down and worshiped him. Then, opening their treasures, they offered him gifts, gold and frankincense and myrrh' (Matt. 2:11). God still rewards earnest, persevering seekers after Jesus—those who are truly 'in the business' with Him. Those whose faith is merely nominal, however, are strangers to true Christian blessing. God states in His Word, 'You will seek me and find me; when you seek me with all your heart' (Jer. 29:13).

Fourthly, the prayer mentions *the obedience of Joseph and Mary*. Joseph and Mary, of course, figure prominently in the Christmas story—although even they take second place to Christ. As we saw in Chapter 13, little is said about Joseph in the Bible. After receiving angelic assurance that Mary's conception of Christ was by the Holy Spirit, he provided background support for his wife-to-be. Mary herself gives us an example to emulate in that she submitted meekly to the will of God. When the angel Gabriel explained to her that, of all the women in the world, she alone was to be the one who would give birth to the longed-for Messiah, after initial fear and puzzlement she said, 'Behold, I am the handmaid of the Lord; let it be to me according to your word' (Luke 1:38). God's will is always best. Knowing, obeying and submitting to the will of God is surely the secret of true happiness.

Lastly, the prayer mentions *the peace of the Christ-child*. The best has been saved for last. Isaiah's ancient prophecy describes Jesus as 'the Prince of peace' (Isa. 9:6). Colossians 1:20 explains His 'making peace by the blood of his cross'. The Christ of Bethlehem alone can give sinners peace with God. Our sin alienates us from Him and puts us under His wrath. But the Christ of Bethlehem grew up to become the Christ of Calvary. He lived a sinless life and at Calvary died an atoning death. He reconciles to God every sinner who believes in Him—who avails themselves of His atoning work. So Wesley was spot on when he wrote 'Hail the heaven-born Prince of peace!' and 'Peace on earth, and mercy mild, God and sinners reconciled!'[1] Christ's cradle was with a view to His cross. He was born to die. He was born to reconcile sinners to God. When our faith is in the Lord Jesus Christ, the peace of God becomes ours—eternally. Romans 5:1 declares, 'Therefore, since we are justified by faith, we have peace with God through our Lord Jesus Christ.'

So my prayer for you is the prayer we have just considered. If this prayer is answered in you, you will have a truly happy Christmas, for the blessing of the Christ of Christmas will be yours now, and will remain yours for ever. So let us read the prayer again now as we close:

> May the joy of the angels, the eagerness of the
> shepherds, the perseverance of the wise men,
> the obedience of Joseph and Mary and the peace
> of the Christ-child be yours this Christmas;
> and the blessing of God Almighty, the Father,

the Son and the Holy Spirit, be among you
and remain with you always. Amen.

Reflect on these points

1. *True Christmas joy—and true Christian joy—is knowing Jesus as our own personal Saviour: being a beneficiary of His saving work, and receiving through Him the forgiveness of our sins and the consequent peace with God and sure hope of eternal life.*

2. *There is an urgency about the message of salvation, for salvation is the most crucial matter of all. Our attitude towards Jesus actually determines where we will spend eternity.*

3. *God's will is always best. Knowing, obeying and submitting to the will of God is surely the secret of true happiness.*

Merry Christmas and a Happy New Year!

Part 2: And a happy New Year

The unknown year ahead

As we approach the unknown year ahead, I am reminded of the following hymn which is especially helpful and applicable for such a time:

> God holds the key of all unknown,
> And I am glad;
> If other hands should hold the key,
> Or if He trusted it to me,
> I might be sad.
>
> What if tomorrow's cares were here
> Without its rest?
> I'd rather He unlocked the day;
> And, as the hours swing open, say,
> 'My will is best.'
>
> I cannot read His future plans;
> But this I know:
> I have the smiling of His face,
> And all the refuge of His grace,
> While here below.[1]

Truth be told, it is a great mercy that Almighty God doesn't reveal to us all the details of what lies ahead in our lives. Who would have thought that being limited in knowledge is a blessing? But it certainly is as we stand on the threshold of a new year. Imagine if all of last year's ups and downs, successes and failures, good health and ill health, joys and sorrows, trials and tribulations, and pleasures, pains and perplexities had been shown to us all at once on 31 December . . . We would all surely swoon instantly. Ignorance is not always bliss, but it certainly is in this sphere.

Divine omniscience

Our ignorance of the future, however, does not detract from God's omniscience. He is all-knowing. He alone knows 'the end from the beginning and from ancient times things not yet done' (Isa. 46:10). He alone can say to His people, 'For I know the plans I have for you, says the LORD, plans for welfare and not for evil, to give you a future and a hope' (Jer. 29:11). There are no unforeseen circumstances, unexpected surprises or hidden things with Almighty God! This fact should encourage us to trust Him day by day. 'He knows the way that I take' (Job 23:10). 'His understanding is beyond measure' (Ps. 147:5).

> Even before a word is on my tongue,
>> lo, O LORD, thou knowest it altogether.
> Thou dost beset me behind and before,
>> and layest thy hand upon me.
> (Ps. 139:4–5)

From fear to faith

If we look out, look within and look ahead, naturally, the prospect of the New Year can seem quite terrifying. But the Christian may take heart from knowing that God is already where we are going! In Revelation 1:8 He says, 'I am the Alpha and the Omega . . . who is and who was and who is to come, the Almighty.' And in Revelation 22:13 the Lord Jesus Christ, evidencing His co-equality with God, pronounces likewise: 'I am the Alpha and the Omega, the first and the last, the beginning and the end.'

The antidote to fear of the unknown, therefore, is faith—or, more specifically, faith in the God revealed in the Bible. David, a man who certainly knew the meaning of turmoil, said this in Psalm 31:14–15: 'But I trust in thee, O LORD, I say, "Thou art my God." My times are in thy hand.' And during a particularly tumultuous time he wrote in Psalm 56:3–4:

> When I am afraid,
>> I put my trust in thee.
> In God, whose word I praise,
>> in God I trust without a fear.
>> What can flesh do to me?

Notice David's stress on God's Word here. It is God's Word, the Bible, wherein we find God's unbreakable promises of all-sufficient grace—His saving grace and His sustaining grace. His saving grace is revealed in His provision of His Son to be our Saviour: if we have been redeemed by the blood of Christ, all is eternally well with our souls. But the Bible also reveals the sustaining grace of God: 'My grace is sufficient for you' (2 Cor. 12:9). It has been well said that 'God's grace keeps pace with whatever we face.' Indeed, the Bible assures God's children that He is actually ordering all of our circumstances for the ultimate blessing and well-being of His children (see Rom. 8:28).

So we do not know what the year ahead holds for us—but God does, for He is already there. We may safely entrust the unknown year to a known God—the God and Father of our Lord Jesus Christ. He is infinite in wisdom, compassion, mercy and righteousness. He is all-wise, all-loving, all-sovereign, unstoppable and unthwartable as regards fulfilling His purposes of grace and glory, to the praise of His name. How we need to trust Him more than we do!

> I know who holds the future,
> And He'll guide me with His hand;
> With God things don't just happen,
> Everything by Him is planned.
> So as I face tomorrow,
> With its problems large and small,
> I'll trust the God of miracles,
> Give to Him my all.[2]

Reflect on these points

1. *It is a great mercy that Almighty God doesn't reveal to us all the details of what lies ahead in our lives. But God is all-knowing. There are no unforeseen circumstances, unexpected surprises or hidden things with Him!*

2. *If we look out, look within and look ahead, naturally, the prospect of the New Year can seem quite terrifying. But the Christian may take heart from knowing that God is already where we are going!*

3. *The antidote to fear of the unknown is faith in the God*

revealed in the Bible. We may safely entrust the unknown year to a known God—the God and Father of our Lord Jesus Christ.

Fear not!

I am told—although I have not counted them personally—that there are 366 'Fear not's or their equivalent in the Bible. That is a 'Fear not' for every day of the year, including a leap year.

If we are honest, we would all have to confess that we are no strangers to fear, even if our reasons for fear vary. Well-meaning friends, of course, often tell us not to fear or worry. At such times, though, we might wonder how they would react if they were going through what we are going through. Circumstances can at times seem overwhelming. Circumstances can give us reason to fear.

But the 'Fear not's of the Bible are no mere empty platitudes. For attached to each of these 'Fear not's is a promise which gives us the reason why we need not fear. We will consider some of these now. They are a welcome word as we approach the unknown future.

Father Abraham

The first recorded 'Fear not' with a promise attached in the Bible is in Genesis 15:1, where God Himself says to Abram: 'Fear not, Abram, I am your shield.' Old Abram at this time had every reason to fear. He had just returned from a battle against an alliance of kings. He had been victorious, but perhaps now there was an aftermath. He was no doubt fatigued, and perhaps he feared reprisals. But Almighty God said to him, 'Fear not, Abram, I am your shield.' And because of the knowledge that Almighty God was His sovereign, omnipotent protector, Abram's fears vanished.

The good news is that, if we belong to Jesus, we too may

know Abram's divine shield, for the New Testament says that Christians are Abraham's spiritual descendants, and thus may know and enjoy all the spiritual benefits Abraham enjoyed. 'And if you are Christ's, then you are Abraham's offspring, heirs according to promise' (Gal. 3:29).

> A sovereign Protector I have,
> Unseen, yet for ever at hand,
> Unchangeably faithful to save,
> Almighty to rule and command.
> He smiles, and my comforts abound;
> His grace as the dew shall descend;
> And walls of salvation surround
> The soul He delights to defend.[1]

The fear of judgement

What of the fear of God's judgement? What of the fear of facing God in the life to come? The Bible says, 'It is appointed for men to die once, and after that comes judgment' (Heb. 9:27). We know our own hearts, and we know that we are guilty sinners in His sight. Being cast into eternal hell is a fear we have every reason to hold when we admit who we are in the sight of God . . .

But the merciful promise of God in Christ is able to banish this fear! There is a gospel remedy! God says in Isaiah 43:1, 'Fear not, for I have redeemed you; I have called you by name, you are mine.' Christians do not, and need not, fear the judgement to come, not because of who we are, but because of what God in Christ has done. Christ has redeemed us from our sin and condemnation. He has set us free by paying the price for our sins Himself—by being punished in our room and stead on Calvary's cross. The gospel assures us that 'In him we have redemption through his blood, the forgiveness of our trespasses, according to the riches of his grace.'

Fear of the future
The promises of God banish our fears for the future. The unknown way—what might be—holds many fears. Will we be able to cope in the future? Will our resources be sufficient? Will the trials and sorrows of earth overwhelm us? No. For the promise of God in Isaiah 41:10 is true. There He says to His children,

> Fear not, for I am with you,
>> be not dismayed, for I am your God;
> I will strengthen you, I will help you,
>> I will uphold you with my victorious right hand.

Here we are promised God's presence and power. He will never fail us nor forsake us. His sufficiency will be more than adequate for our insufficiency. His strength will compensate for our weakness when we trust Him for His grace.

He cares about you
Finally, in Luke 12:7, the Lord Jesus says to His own, 'Fear not; you are of more value than many sparrows.' In Matthew 10:29 Jesus explained, 'Are not two sparrows sold for a penny?

And not one of them will fall to the ground without your Father's will.' Here the Saviour is telling us that we need not fear because God our Father is in total control. He is reasoning from the lesser to the greater. If even an insignificant sparrow cannot die apart from the will of God, how much more are the lives, deaths and everything in between of His blood-bought children under God's sovereign superintendence, loving care and total control!

So *fear not*. Our God reigns. He is looking after you. He is watching over you. 'He cares about you' (1 Peter 5:7). He is working through and weaving together all the intricate details of His children's lives for their eternal good and eternal glory. A true fear—that is, respect and honour—and love of this God are the antidote to all our fears!

> Fear Him, ye saints, and you will then
> Have nothing else to fear;
> Make you His service your delight,
> Your wants shall be His care.[2]

How we need to trust Him and His sovereign love more than we do! Our God has not vacated His throne, and He never will!

> There's not a particle of dust can fly,
> A sparrow fall, or cloud obscure the sky,
> A moth be crushed, or leaf fall from a tree,
> But in submission to His wise decree.
>
> He must and will at all times keep in view
> His glory, and His people's welfare too;

Bright days, dark nights, the furious or the flood,
He overrules for Zion's real good.[3]

Reflect on these points

1. *Being cast into eternal hell is a fear we have every reason to hold when we admit who we are in the sight of God. But there is a gospel remedy! Christians need not fear the judgement to come, not because of who we are, but because of what God in Christ has done.*

2. *We are promised God's presence and power. He will never fail us nor forsake us. His sufficiency will be more than adequate for our insufficiency. His strength will compensate for our weakness when we trust Him for His grace.*

3. *If even an insignificant sparrow cannot die apart from the will of God, how much more are the lives, deaths and everything in between of His blood-bought children under God's sovereign superintendence, loving care and total control!*

God is in control

In this tumultuous and stormy world of ours, the Christian is both advised and exhorted to think biblically and to remember that, contrary to appearances at times, God is on the throne, and as such is in total control of all things. 'The LORD has established his throne in the heavens, and his kingdom rules over all' (Ps. 103:19).

Nothing seems more lawless, destructive and out of control than a storm at sea. But Scripture teaches that God is in control of the mighty waves. He is almighty. Psalm 89:9 reads, 'Thou dost rule the raging of the sea; when its waves rise, thou stillest them.' Why doesn't the sea engulf us land-dwellers in one giant tsunami? The Bible's answer is, 'Because it is controlled by God.' He has, says Job 38:8–10, 'shut in the sea with doors . . . and prescribed bounds for it, and set bars and doors, and said, "Thus far shall you come, and no farther, and here shall your proud waves be stayed."'

Truth be told, the only ultimate comfort we have is that our God—our loving heavenly Father—is absolutely sovereign. He is in total control of all things.

God is in control of the devil

Consider first of all God's control in relation to Satan, our arch-enemy. Scripture reveals that we have an enemy who is opposed both to us and to God. The devil seeks to cause us havoc and misery, and he is more powerful, more intelligent and more cunning than we will ever be. But Scripture teaches that even the devil is subject to God's control and is a pawn in

His hand. Satan is mighty, but God is almighty. Satan can only touch and buffet us as much as God sees fit for our blessing!

We see this in the book of Job. Job was sorely tried and tested by Satan—but only within the bounds prescribed by God Himself. God permitted Satan to take away Job's family and worldly possessions, and to inflict him with a painful physical affliction. But God did not allow Satan to kill Job. Under the absolute sovereignty of God, Job came through his trial. Job's faith proved true and his trust in God was well founded. Job testified of God, 'But he knows the way that I take; when he has tried me, I shall come forth as gold' (Job 23:10).

Amazingly, God even uses evil to His greater glory. Witness the most evil act of all, namely the crucifixion of His Son. This was an act of wicked men, but also an act of God—His provision of a sinless sacrifice to atone for the sins of His people. Acts 2:23 reminds us that 'Jesus, delivered up according to the definite plan and foreknowledge of God, [was] crucified and killed by the hands of lawless men'.

God is in control of our salvation

Consider, secondly, Christian conversion. Why doesn't God let us continue our lives as we started, in Christ-less unbelief, going our own way? Answer: He has prescribed a limit to our unbelief. He foreordained the day of our birth, and He foreordained the day of our new birth. He allowed us to live our own way, on the way to destruction, only for so long. Then His grace arrested us. He was in sovereign control. Salvation is all of God's sovereign grace. There is nothing accidental about it. Looking beyond all secondary causes, no one has ever stumbled accidentally on Christ! Salvation is an act of God—a gracious divine intervention in a person's life, according to God's predestined plan. He saves some early in their lives. He saves some later. Some are from Christian homes. Some are not. God is God. His will, will be done. A Christian is a Christian because, 1 Peter 1:2 tells us, he or she has been 'chosen and destined by God the Father and sanctified by the Spirit for obedience to Jesus Christ and for sprinkling with his blood'.

God is in control of our death

Thirdly, consider our last enemy—another one who is more powerful than we are, and who is in control of us, not us of him. This is death itself. We have no say in the matter. We could die at birth. We could die because of an illness. We could die because of a terrorist incident. We could die because of a road accident. We could die in old age . . . But Scripture teaches that God Himself has foreordained the exact moment of our death. We are immortal until our work is done! We will not die prematurely, and we will not breathe for a moment longer than God has seen fit. He has foreordained both the day of our birth and the day of our death. God Himself both has set and is safeguarding the limits to our lives. 'My times are in thy hand' (Ps. 31:15).

> Thy eyes beheld my unformed substance;
> in thy book were written, every one of them,

> the days that were formed for me,
>
> > when as yet there was none of them.
>
> (Ps. 139:16)

The day of the Christian's death is foreordained. And death for the Christian will be the porter who ushers us into the nearer presence of God Himself!

So take comfort, then, from the ultimate comfort: the comfort of having and knowing a sovereign God. He rules and overrules—even over evil? Yes, even over evil. Our conversion to Christ was subject to His sovereignty. Our very lives are subject to His sovereignty, as is our entrance into the life to come. 'Hallelujah! For the Lord our God the Almighty reigns' (Rev. 19:6).

> This is my Father's world:
>
> O let me ne'er forget
>
> That though the wrong seems oft so strong,
>
> God is the ruler yet.
>
> This is my Father's world:
>
> Why should my heart be sad?
>
> The Lord is King: let the heavens ring!
>
> God reigns; let earth be glad![1]

Reflect on these points

1. *The ultimate comfort we have is that our God—our loving heavenly Father—is absolutely sovereign. He is in total control of all things.*

2. *Even the devil is subject to God's control and is a pawn in His hand. Satan is mighty, but God is almighty. Satan can only touch and buffet us as much as God sees fit for our blessing!*

3. *God has foreordained the exact moment of our death. We are immortal until our work is done! We will not die prematurely, and we will not breathe for a moment longer than God has seen fit.*

A storm at sea

On the wall in my hall I have a quite spectacular framed photo of the breakwater at Porthcawl Point, on the South Wales coast. The photograph was taken during an exceptional winter storm. Central to the picture is a wave hitting the breakwater and sending a fountain of foamy white spray some eighty feet up into the air. Visitors tell me that the photograph is both exciting and terrifying. It captures something of the awesome power of the elements—a power far greater than us, and far beyond our control. The sea which surrounds our British Isles holds both delights and dangers.

Can we, though, draw any spiritual lessons from my photo of a stormy day at Porthcawl—lessons which will encourage us as we step out into a new year? I believe we can. The big waves of that day teach us lessons about both the greatness and the grace of God.

The greatness of God

In Psalm 93:3–4 we read,

> The floods have lifted up, O LORD,
>   the floods have lifted up their voice,
>   the floods lift up their roaring.
> Mightier than the thunders of many waters,
>   mightier than the waves of the sea,
>   the LORD on high is mighty!

These verses are a welcome reminder of the greatness and power of God. We can safely state that God is always greater than all of our troubles. Our troubles are large to us, but they are small to God. The problems, difficulties and trials we now face and which we will face in the future in this fallen world are certainly great, vexing and perplexing. But God is greater than them all. He is almighty. He is 'El Shaddai', God Almighty.

What a blessing and a comfort it is to know that, if we belong to Jesus, we have access to this God who has the solution to all our difficulties, and who has promised to send us His all-sufficient grace and help when we call upon Him. Take courage from the greatness of God. Strive for a divine perspective. Ponder the psalm again: 'Mightier than the thunders of many waters, mightier than the waves of the sea, the LORD on high is mighty!' A Sunday school chorus runs 'My God is so big, so strong and so mighty, there's nothing that He cannot do.' That chorus is in line with the Bible. For the God of the Bible is both sovereign and omnipotent. Jeremiah 32:17, for instance, reads, 'Ah Lord God! It is thou who hast made the heavens and the earth by thy great power and by thy outstretched arm! Nothing is too hard for thee.'

Secondly, the winter storm at Porthcawl reminds us of:

The grace of God

Did you know that the Bible uses the imagery of a frightening, destructive storm to depict something of God's wrath, His holy indignation against sinners? God is a holy God. Sin is an affront to Him, and He can only react to it in judgement. Hence Jeremiah 23:19 reads,

Behold, the storm of the LORD!
  Wrath has gone forth,
a whirling tempest;
  it will burst upon the head of the wicked.

We all know that we have displeased God in some way or other. We have all done things He has forbidden, and we have not always done what He has commanded. As the Book of Common Prayer puts it: 'We have left undone those things which we ought to have done, and we have done those things which we ought not to have done.' We have made ourselves liable to the frightening wrath of God.

The biggest question of all is: Can we ever escape from the impending storm of God's wrath against us? The answer of the Bible is that we can! And we can do so by the grace of God in Christ at Calvary. We have a gospel of grace to embrace and proclaim!

At Calvary, Jesus stood in the sinner's place and weathered the storm of God's wrath to save us from it. The Psalms prophesied of that time. Taking us to an 'insider's view' of Calvary, we read, 'all thy waves and thy billows have gone over me' (Ps. 42:7), and 'Thy wrath lies heavy upon me, and thou dost overwhelm me with all thy waves' (Ps. 88:7). These psalms have their ultimate fulfilment in Christ, when He died at Calvary and bore the wrath of God, the most terrifying divine storm, against sins not His own, so that we might be saved: so that God's wrath might be turned aside from us, and we might have peace with God and be assured, through faith in Christ, of a home in the eternal haven of heaven by and by. The Christian gospel is the Good News of salvation. Salvation means 'rescue' or 'deliverance'. A rescue or deliverance from what? From the terrifying wrath of God.

There are, then, two vital lessons from a stormy day at the seaside, with its strong winds and huge waves. If we have eyes to see it, that exciting and frightening day gives us a welcome reminder of both the greatness of God and the grace of God. The Good News is that Christ braved the storm for me to make my peace with God!

> The tempest's awful voice was heard,
> O Christ, it broke on Thee!
> Thy open bosom was my ward,
> It braved the storm for me;
> Thy form was scarred, Thy visage marred,
> Now cloudless peace for me.[1]

Reflect on these points

1. *The problems, difficulties and trials we now face and which we will face in the future in this fallen world are certainly great, vexing and perplexing. But God is greater than them all.*

2. *We have all displeased God in some way or other. We have all done things He has forbidden, and we have not always done what He has commanded. Can we ever escape from the impending storm of God's wrath against us? The answer of the Bible is that we can!*

3. When Christ died at Calvary He bore the wrath of God, the most terrifying divine storm, against sins not His own, so that God's wrath might be turned aside from us, and we might have peace with God and be assured of a home in the eternal haven of heaven by and by.

One day at
a time

Fear not tomorrow, child of the King,

Leave it to Jesus, and do the next thing.[1]

Standing on the brink of a new year can be a daunting, even intimidating, experience. If we are not careful, our imaginations can go into overdrive, and we can be gripped by fear. What awaits me in the unknown year? Will my health stand up? Will my finances be adequate? How will I cope with a sudden calamity? What of my loved ones? . . .

How then are we to approach a new year, with our miscellaneous fears of 'what might be'? Well, according to the Lord Jesus, we are to approach a new year, and life itself, taking just one day at a time.

In Matthew 6:34 the Saviour gives us a kindly exhortation. Having just emphasized God the Father's providential care and provision for His children, He says, 'Therefore do not be anxious about tomorrow, for tomorrow will be anxious for itself. Let the day's own trouble be sufficient for the day.'

According to the Lord Jesus, then, we are not to be unduly anxious about the days ahead. To do so shows an implicit *distrust* of our Father's love and care. Rather, we are to take life one day at a time as God's providence unfolds, and deal with the immediate tasks we have in hand.

Make preparation?

Whilst the Bible forbids anxiety about the future, at the same time it does not forbid us to make preparation and provision for the future. In fact, it exhorts us to be prudent. In Proverbs 6:6–8, for example, we are urged to emulate the ant!

> Go to the ant . . .
>> consider her ways, and be wise.
> Without having any chief,
>> officer or ruler,
> she prepares her food in summer,
>> and gathers her sustenance in harvest.

Then in Proverbs 10:5 we are told, 'A son who gathers in summer is prudent.' By implication, we can say that savings, insurance and a pension plan are by no means contrary to the will of God. No. Whilst the Bible exhorts us to prepare and be prepared for the future, what the Bible prohibits is undue anxiety about the future. Our future is securely in the hands of the eternal God. He will lead us to this one day at a time, according to His plan, as His providence unfolds.

Standing on the brink

So on the brink of an unknown year, heed the words of the Son of God: 'Do not be anxious about tomorrow, for tomorrow will be anxious for itself. Let the day's own trouble be sufficient for the day.' Jesus is saying words to the effect of 'Don't fret and worry about the future. Do what you know you ought to do today. The future is God's responsibility, not yours. He has promised to be with you each step of your life. What more could you ask for?'

Grace for each day

God's grace cannot be hoarded or given in advance. He gives us strength sufficient for the day—for the present, and not for tomorrow. Deuteronomy 33:25 promises, 'As your days, so shall your strength be.'

It is noteworthy that Jesus encouraged us to pray to God, 'Give us *this day* our daily bread' (Matt. 6:11). In doing so, he was encouraging us to trust God to provide for our needs just one day at a time. This reminds us of the occasion when God provided for His people in the barren wilderness in Old Testament times. The wilderness was a dead place, incapable of sustaining life. But God provided manna from heaven for His people, and He did so day by day: 'Morning by morning they gathered it' (Exod. 16:21). God provided them with daily bread, but when some tried to hoard it for the future, Exodus 16:20 tells us that 'it bred worms and became foul'.

So, according to the Lord Jesus, we are to face the future with confidence in God's undertaking, and tackle the future just one day at a time. We are not to be unduly anxious about our unknown tomorrows, but seek God's help to cope with the present task and circumstances He has given us. The God of the Bible is infinitely worthy of our trust. He is at the helm of His children's lives. He has promised to provide for all our needs and to bestow His all-sufficient grace and strength to enable us to cope with our particular and peculiar circumstances. As we face a new year, then, let us remember the words of the Son of God. In the light of God's goodness, 'do not be anxious about tomorrow, for tomorrow will be anxious for itself. Let the day's own trouble be sufficient for the day.'

The hymnwriter must have had those words in mind when he wrote:

> I have nothing to do with tomorrow,
> My Saviour will make that His care;
> Should He fill it with trouble and sorrow,
> He'll help me to suffer and bear.
>
> I have nothing to do with tomorrow,
> Its burdens then why should I share?
> Its grace and its faith I can't borrow,
> Then why should I borrow its care?[2]

Reflect on these points

1. *To be unduly anxious about the days ahead shows an implicit distrust of our Father's love and care.*

2. *The Bible does not forbid us to make preparation and provision for the future; what the Bible prohibits is undue anxiety about the future.*

3. *God's grace cannot be hoarded or given in advance. He gives us strength sufficient for the day—for the present, and not for tomorrow. We are to face the future with confidence in God's undertaking, and tackle it just one day at a time.*

Big Ben

For those who live in the UK, New Year's Eve is synonymous with the chimes of Big Ben at 11.59 p.m. on 31 December—although at the time of writing it is currently silent due to renovation work. Big Ben is one of the iconic landmarks of the UK. I'm biased, as when I was eight years old, my father and I were taken up Big Ben. We climbed the tower's 334 steps—it has no lift. With hindsight, I realize that I was very privileged. Security being what it is today, the general public are prohibited from going up Big Ben now.

'Big Ben' technically refers to the 13.5-ton bell housed in what used to be called St Stephen's Tower (now called the Elizabeth Tower) on the north-east end of the Palace of Westminster in London. The name, though, has become synonymous with the 96.3-metre-high, four-faced tower which houses the great bell.

Can we glean any spiritual lessons from Big Ben? I believe we can.

The preaching of the gospel

Big Ben's 13.5-ton bell, when struck by a huge, mechanical hammer each hour, has an unmistakable sound. We had to cover our ears when we stood by it. On a clear night, the guards at Windsor Castle are able to hear it, and they are some twenty-five miles away. All this is comparable with the preaching of the gospel.

In 1 Thessalonians 1:8 Paul reminded the Thessalonians how 'the word of the Lord sounded forth from you'. Almighty God ensures that His elect will hear the gospel of salvation and believe. God, by His Spirit, through His Word, makes His people hear. In the ears of God's elect, the gospel will have an unmistakable sound, and the ring of truth and authenticity that it is nothing less than the voice of God Himself speaking.

The kingdom of heaven is furthered by the preaching of the gospel. The gospel is 'the power of God for salvation to every one who has faith' (Rom. 1:16). Romans 10:17 tells us that 'faith comes from what is heard, and what is heard comes by the preaching of Christ'.

The New Testament verb 'to preach' means 'to herald forth'. Through the heralding forth—the sounding out—of the gospel of Christ, sinners are saved. God uses means. Through preaching, sinners are convicted of their sin and lost plight, shown the crucified Christ as the answer to their need, and enabled to cleave to Him for full and eternal salvation.

Big Ben's chimes, then, remind us of the preaching of the gospel. 'We preach Christ crucified' (1 Cor. 1:23).

> The Gospel bells are ringing,
> Over land, from sea to sea:
> Blessed news of free salvation
> Do they offer you and me.
> For God so loved the world
> That His only Son He gave;
> Whosoe'er believeth in Him
> Everlasting life shall have.[1]

The providence of God

Big Ben reminds us also of God's providence. In Psalm 31:15 David looked up to heaven and said, 'My times are in thy hand.' Knowing that our times are in God's hand is a great comfort to the soul. If our times really are in God's hand, we can safely leave them there. He is the sovereign God. There are no 'accidents' in His children's lives. He has everything under control. He knows how to tailor and taper our circumstances for our eternal good, and He is doing so. He is working out the intricate details of our lives according to His eternal plan for our good and His glory. 'For from him and through him and to him are all things. To him be glory for ever. Amen' (Rom. 11:36).

As the hands of Big Ben turn inexorably, then, and the hours pass by, how good it is to be able to make David's confession our own, and say to God: 'My times are in Thy hand.'

> My times are in Thy hand,
> Whatever they may be;
> Pleasing or painful, dark or bright,
> As best may seem to Thee.
>
> My times are in Thy hand;
> Why should I doubt or fear?
> A Father's hand will never cause
> His child a needless tear.[2]

Great is Thy faithfulness

Big Ben reminds us also of the reliability and dependability of

Almighty God, and how infinitely worthy He is of our trust. Big Ben is famous for its reliability. We are told that Londoners set their watches and clocks by it. Yet the clock has had one or two hitches over the last century and a half of its existence. Some heavy snow once slowed its hands down so that it gave the incorrect time. It has also known mechanical failures—wear and tear—which have needed to be fixed.

The God of the Bible, however, never fails His people. He is always faithful to His promises. Psalm 100:5 tells us, 'The LORD is good; his steadfast love endures for ever, and his faithfulness to all generations.' Lamentations 3:22–23 affirms:

> The steadfast love of the LORD never ceases,
>> his mercies never come to an end;
> they are new every morning;
>> great is thy faithfulness.

The brevity of time

Lastly, Big Ben sounds out a warning to us. It reminds us all that time is short. Job spoke for us all when he said, 'My days are swifter than a weaver's shuttle' (Job 7:6). The hands of Big Ben may have stopped sometimes, but time itself is unstoppable. We are all heading for eternity. The psalmist said, 'Man is like a breath, his days are like a passing shadow' (Ps. 144:4). This being so, the most important question we can ask ourselves is: 'Where will I spend eternity?' The Bible would have us all hold in mind the brevity of time, the nearness of eternity, a heaven to be gained, a hell to be shunned, and a Saviour who really saves.

None of us are promised a tomorrow. How imperative it is, then, that we believe in Jesus, the only Saviour, while we may, before it is too late! The gospel exhortation is to 'Believe in the Lord Jesus, and you will be saved' (Acts 16:31), for 'Behold, now is the acceptable time; behold, now is the day of salvation' (2 Cor. 6:2).

So there is Big Ben, one of the UK's most famous landmarks. It chimes in the New Year each year for many, and it is seen and heard on our TVs and radios most days before the evening news. Heed, though, its spiritual lessons. The gospel of salvation is to be rung out until Jesus comes again; Almighty God is in control of His children's lives and times; the God of the Bible is infinitely reliable and to be trusted; and time is short, eternity is near, and Jesus is the only Saviour. He saves for time and eternity.

> Time is gliding swiftly by,
> Death and judgment draweth nigh,
> To the arms of Jesus fly,
> Be in time.
> Oh, I pray you count the cost,
> Ere the fatal line be crossed,
> And your soul in hell be lost,
> Be in time.[3]

Final note: Interestingly, there is a plaque in the clock room of Big Ben on which is some verse based on Psalm 37:23–24.

The verse may be said in time to Big Ben's quarter bell chimes. It reads:

> All through this hour
> Lord be my guide
> And by Thy power
> No foot shall slide.

Reflect on these points

1. *Almighty God ensures that His elect will hear the gospel of salvation and believe. In the ears of God's elect, the gospel will have an unmistakable sound, and the ring of truth and authenticity that it is nothing less than the voice of God Himself speaking.*

2. *If our times really are in God's hand, we can safely leave them there. There are no 'accidents' in His children's lives. He has everything under control.*

3. *Time is unstoppable. We are all heading for eternity. None of us are promised a tomorrow. How imperative it is that we believe in Jesus, the only Saviour, while we may, before it is too late!*

'Have Thine own way, Lord'

How do you cope—and how will you cope—with terrible, traumatic and tumultuous days in your life? We all have had them. We all have them. And we all will have them. A sudden, unwanted change comes our way. A cherished plan and hope is dashed and fails to come to fruition. We experience failure, frustration or humiliation. We have a sudden calamity or loss.

The Bible's answer is that we should submit. Or, rather, the Bible's answer is that we should submit to the sovereign will of God and say with Eli, 'It is the LORD; let him do what seems good to him' (1 Sam. 3:18).

Seeing the hand of God in everything that happens to us changes our perspective. Deuteronomy 32:4 reminds us that, whatever our feelings may be, 'His work is perfect; for all his ways are justice. A God of faithfulness and without iniquity, just and right is he.' Genesis 18:25 says, 'Shall not the Judge of all the earth do right?' God has His sovereign will and overall plan for our lives. It is described in Romans 12:2 as 'good and acceptable and perfect'. Who are we to question His wisdom, and how—especially in the light of the cross of Christ—can we ever doubt His love? He knows what is best for us, as He knows us better than we know ourselves. Hence we can echo Job 2:10: 'Shall we receive good at the hand of God, and shall we not receive evil?'

The heavenly Potter

In Isaiah 64:8 we read, 'O LORD, thou art our Father; we are the clay, and thou art our potter.' This being so, can we not view the pressures, pain and perplexity of life as coming from the hands of the loving heavenly Potter? He is making and moulding a vessel after His own will: a vessel destined to be like Jesus, a vessel destined for glory.

Just as it is absurd for the clay to dictate to the potter what to do, so it is absurd for us to dictate to Almighty God what He ought to do. Isaiah 45:9 warns,

> Woe to him who strives with his Maker,
>> an earthen vessel with the potter!
> Does the clay say to him who fashions it, 'What are
>> you making?'
>> or 'Your work has no handles'?

Isaiah 45:11 says,

> Thus says the LORD,
>> the Holy One of Israel, and his Maker:
> 'Will you question me about my children,
>> or command me concerning the work of my hands?'

Your will be done

Back in 1907, one Adelaide Pollard was convinced that the Lord had called her to be a missionary in Africa. However, the funds needed to accomplish what she believed to be God's will for her life failed to come in, and her plans to be a missionary in Africa were thwarted. Puzzled and perplexed at the providence of God, she attended a church prayer meeting. Whilst there she overheard an elderly woman pray: 'It's all right, Lord. It doesn't matter what you bring into our lives. Just have Your own way with us.' Picking up on that prayer 'Have Your own way with us, Lord', Adelaide Pollard was inspired to write the following hymn—a hymn which gave her comfort and reassurance in her disappointment, and one which has given comfort and reassurance to God's people for the past hundred years:

> Have Thine own way, Lord!
> Have Thine own way!
> Thou art the Potter,
> I am the clay.
> Mould me and make me
> After Thy will,
> While I am waiting,
> Yielded and still.
>
> Have Thine own way, Lord!
> Have Thine own way!
> Search me and try me,
> Master today!
> Whiter than snow, Lord,
> Wash me just now,
> As in Thy presence
> Humbly I bow.
>
> Have Thine own way, Lord!
> Have Thine own way!
> Wounded and weary,

Help me I pray!
Power, all power,
Surely is Thine!
Touch me and heal me,
Saviour divine!

Have Thine own way, Lord!
Have Thine own way!
Hold o'er my being
Absolute sway.
Fill with Thy Spirit
Till all shall see
Christ only, always,
Living in me!

Whatever our circumstances, then, let us look to God. He is able, and He will work out all things for the ultimate blessing of His children and the glory of His name. He knows what He is doing. With Him there are no disappointments—only eternal plans to fulfil. We will end by agreeing with Psalm 138:8: 'The LORD will fulfil his purpose for me; thy steadfast love, O LORD, endures for ever. Do not forsake the work of thy hands.'

Reflect on these points

1. *Seeing the hand of God in everything that happens to us changes our perspective. Who are we to question His wisdom, and how—especially in the light of the cross of Christ—can we ever doubt His love?*

2. *Just as it is absurd for the clay to dictate to the potter what to do, so it is absurd for us to dictate to Almighty God what He ought to do.*

3. *God knows what He is doing. With Him there are no disappointments—only eternal plans to fulfil.*

The ultimate refuge

The stars in the sky are there all the time, yet we notice them only when night-time comes. It is similar with some of the precious promises contained in the Bible. They are there all the time, but sometimes we only take real notice of them when the dark night of trouble comes upon us. In dark times, the promises of God seem to shine much more brightly; having a need and a vested interest in them, the believer takes much more notice of them, and finds them much more delightful.

One such precious promise is Psalm 46:1. This affirms, 'God is our refuge and strength, a very present help in trouble.' The verse needs a half-hour sermon to unlock. But, in a nutshell, it tells us that in God we have:

- A *powerful refuge:* for '*God*', the Creator of the universe, 'is our refuge and strength'.
- A *present refuge:* for He is '*a very present* help in trouble'.
- A *pertinent refuge:* for He is there just when we need Him as 'a very present *help in trouble*', that is, in and during those circumstances which are beyond our ability and capability.

What is a refuge?

A refuge means a safe hiding place. When the late Christian Corrie ten Boom was imprisoned by the Nazis, she found herself in a solitary prison cell. The cell was dark with dirty water on the floor. Hearing the cries of other prisoners, she feared that she was next in line for torture. She testified: 'Once I stood with my back against the wall with my hands spread out as if to try to push away the walls that were closing in on me. I was dead scared. I cried out, "Lord, I'm not strong enough to endure this. I don't have the faith."'[1]

Corrie thus admitted to a weak faith. But God spoke to her in an unusual way. She noticed an ant on the floor. The moment the ant felt the water, it ran straight to its tiny ant hole in the wall. Corrie explained:

> Then it was as if the Lord said to me, 'What about that ant? He didn't stop to look at the wet floor or his weak feet. He went straight to his hiding place. Corrie. Don't look at your faith. It is weak . . . I am your hiding place and you can come running to Me just like that ant disappeared into that hole in the wall.'

Look up!

In troublesome, volatile times, then, our focus is not to be on our circumstances or on our faith or lack of faith, but on God Himself. As that ant ran to its hole in the wall, so you and I, if we belong to Jesus, may run to our Father in heaven. In fact, He invites us and encourages us to do this. In Psalm 50:15 He says, 'Call upon me in the day of trouble; I will deliver you, and you shall glorify me.'

A refuge, as we have seen, means a safe hiding place. According to the Bible, safety is not the absence of trouble, but the presence of God. He may not see fit to calm our storms or take away our troubles, but in Him we have a safe haven during the storms and troubles. If He doesn't always calm our storms, He knows how to calm His children in the storm. His presence is our peace. He is able to give us peace in a troubled world when He assures us of His love and total control over all things.

How brightly the promises of God in the Bible shine in our darkest days! Read Psalm 46:1 again: 'God is our refuge and strength, a very present help in trouble.'

> Thou art a hiding place for me,
>> thou preservest me from trouble;
>> thou dost encompass me with deliverance.
> (Ps. 32:7)

> The LORD is good,
>> a stronghold in the day of trouble;
>> he knows those who take refuge in him.
> (Nahum 1:7)

God Himself is our ultimate refuge.

> The Lord's our Rock, in Him we hide:
> A shelter in the time of storm;
> Secure, whatever ill betide;
> A shelter in the time of storm.

> *Oh Jesus is a Rock in a weary land,*
> *A shelter in the time of storm.*

> A shade by day, defence by night:
> A shelter in the time of storm;

No fears alarm, no foes affright:
A shelter in the time of storm.

The raging storms may round us beat:
A shelter in the time of storm;
We'll never leave our safe retreat:
A shelter in the time of storm.

A Rock divine, O Refuge dear:
A shelter in the time of storm;
Be Thou our Helper, ever near:
A shelter in the time of storm.[2]

Reflect on these points

1. In troublesome, volatile times, our focus is not to be on our circumstances or on our faith or lack of faith, but on God Himself.

2. Safety is not the absence of trouble, but the presence of God. His presence is our peace.

3. God may not see fit to calm our storms or take away our troubles, but in Him we have a safe haven during the storms and troubles. He Himself is our ultimate refuge.

Romans 8:28

Romans 8:28 reads, 'We know that in everything God works for good with those who love him, who are called according to his purpose.' Here is a verse to really take hold of as we approach the unknown days ahead.

Yet, truth be told, the verse is actually as difficult as it is comforting. It has been of immense comfort to Christians ever since it was penned by divine inspiration, for it reminds us that the events and circumstances of our lives are not accidental but providential—foreordained by God for the ultimate blessing of His children. 'For from him and through him and to him are all things' (Rom. 11:36). The Westminster Shorter Catechism states that 'The decrees of God are His eternal purpose, according to the counsel of His will, whereby, for His own glory, He hath foreordained whatsoever comes to pass' (Question 7).

Yet Romans 8:28 is also a difficult verse. The 'everything' it contains can be hard to believe when we are going through dark times—loss of a job or health, a bereavement, a disappointment, and so on. I recently heard a Christian say, somewhat tongue in cheek, 'Of course, we are all professing Calvinists [that is, professing to believe in the sovereignty of God] until we lose our house keys.' There is truth in the humour, for when we fret and panic we are implicitly saying that Almighty God isn't sovereign and in absolute control of all things.

Romans 8:28 cake

'We know that in everything God works for good with those who love him, who are called according to his purpose.'

Have you ever heard of a 'Romans 8:28 cake'? Every boy thinks that his mother bakes the greatest cakes in the world, and I am no exception. My mother will take flour, eggs, butter, sugar and cocoa powder, mix them together, put the mixture in the oven, and produce the most exquisite chocolate sponge. Yet each ingredient of the cake, when taken on its own, is not very pleasant. No one would eat flour on its own. No one would eat cocoa powder. It is the proportion and mix of all the ingredients together that produces the enjoyable cake.

It is the same with God's dealings with His children. Some of them may seem bitter to the taste. We might wonder whether He has turned up the heat of our lives too high. But He is infinite in wisdom and love. He knows what He is doing. He has our ultimate blessing—our 'good'—in mind. He has an end in view. The losses and crosses of a believer's life are purposeful, not pointless. The God of the Bible is too wise to make mistakes, and too loving to be unkind.

Consider Joseph

A real-life example of Romans 8:28 is Joseph in the Old Testament. Joseph was sold into slavery in Egypt by his jealous brothers. There he went down even further. He was unjustly put in jail. All seemed pointless and against him. But his God-given ability to interpret dreams reached the ears of Pharaoh. Pharaoh was so enamoured with Joseph that he promoted him to second in command in the land. And in such a high position, Joseph, through his foresight, was able to save the people of Israel from dying out due to famine. God's end purpose was thus fulfilled—albeit through Joseph's initial suffering and humiliation. Joseph could therefore testify to his brothers at a later date, 'As for you, you meant evil against me; but God meant it for good, to bring it about that many people should be kept alive, as they are today' (Gen. 50:20). Joseph was really saying the Old Testament equivalent of our verse. 'We know that in everything God works for good with those who love him, who are called according to his purpose.'

So if you, my Christian friend, are currently going through the mill, take heart: God has not abandoned you. He knows what He is doing. Trust Him for His grace. You will yet look back and say with George Mueller, 'My greatest trials have been my greatest blessings.' Or, as the psalmist wrote in Psalm 119:71, 'It is good for me that I was afflicted, that I might learn thy statutes.'

A Christian who knew many dark days and states of mind wrote the following verses. As we approach a new year, and throughout all our years, we would do well to make its sentiments our own.

> Judge not the Lord by feeble sense,
> But trust Him for His grace;
> Behind a frowning providence
> He hides a smiling face.
>
> His purposes will ripen fast,
> Unfolding every hour;

The bud may have a bitter taste,
But sweet will be the flower.

Blind unbelief is sure to err,
And scan His work in vain;
God is His own interpreter,
And He will make it plain.[1]

Reflect on these points

*1. When we fret and panic we are implicitly saying that
Almighty God isn't sovereign and in absolute control of
all things.*

*2. Some of God's dealings with His children may seem
bitter to the taste. But He is infinite in wisdom and love.
He knows what He is doing. And He has our ultimate
blessing—our 'good'—in mind.*

*3. The God of the Bible is too wise to make mistakes, and
too loving to be unkind.*

Divine omnipotence

Did you know that Billy Graham, the late evangelist, once visited South Wales just after the Second World War, before he became world famous? I heard a report about this from someone whose church he visited. Billy Graham's song leader, a genial man called Cliff Barrows, taught them a song which remained with the congregation for the rest of their days. The words went like this:

> Got any rivers you think are uncrossable?
> Got any mountains you can't tunnel through?
> God specializes in things thought impossible,
> And He can do what no other can do.[1]

Almighty God

The song focuses our attention on one of the attributes—that is, characteristics—of the God revealed in the Bible, namely God's omnipotence. The God of the Bible is all-powerful. He is 'El-Shaddai', God Almighty. He is not subject to our human limitations and weaknesses. If we open the Bible anywhere, we are sure to be reminded of God's omnipotence:

> The LORD is the everlasting God,
>> the Creator of the ends of the earth.
> He does not faint or grow weary.
> (Isa. 40:28)

> Ah Lord GOD! It is thou who hast made the heavens
> and the earth by thy great power and by thy

outstretched arm! Nothing is too hard for thee.
(Jer. 32:17)

For with God nothing will be impossible.
(Luke 1:37)

Hallelujah! For the Lord our God the Almighty reigns.
(Rev. 19:6)

As well as using statements and propositions, the Bible reveals God's omnipotence in action. God's omnipotence is such that He created this vast universe by merely speaking it into existence:

By the word of the LORD the heavens were made,
  and all their host by the breath of his mouth . . .
For He spoke, and it came to be;
  he commanded, and it stood forth.
(Ps. 33:6, 9)

God's omnipotence was revealed in Old Testament times when He delivered His people from slavery in Egypt. There seemed to be no escape from Pharaoh's pursuing army as they hunted the Israelites to the banks of the Red Sea. But God intervened and miraculously parted the waters: 'He divided the sea and let them pass through it, and made the waters stand like a heap' (Ps. 78:13).

In New Testament times, God's omnipotence was revealed in the birth of Jesus. Jesus was conceived miraculously, without the instrumentality of a human father. And God's omnipotence, surprisingly, was revealed in the apparent weakness and failure of the cross of Christ, described by Paul as both 'the power of God and the wisdom of God' (1 Cor. 1:24), for the cross of Christ—Christ's dying in the place of sinners—enables God to justly pardon sinners without compromising either His justice or His love.

Have confidence in your God

The God of the Bible, then, is omnipotent. How we must beware of cutting him down to our size to make Him manageable, and of measuring Him by our own puny, human standards. Psalm 93:4 reminds us,

> Mightier than the thunders of many waters,
>   mightier than the waves of the sea,
>   the LORD on high is mighty!

One of the reasons why the Bible keeps reminding us of God's omnipotence is to increase our faith and confidence in Him. God's omnipotence has great pastoral implications. His people need never despair, for this omnipotent God actually condescends to hear the prayers of His children when they come to Him in need, and He then intervenes and gives both His saving and His sustaining grace. 'My help comes from the LORD, who made heaven and earth' (Ps. 121:2).

> Ever cast on Him thy care:
> He invites thee so to do;
> Never let thy soul despair:
> He will surely help thee through.[2]

Remember, then, that God is almighty. No problem is too great for Him. No difficulty is insoluble to Him. No complexity is beyond His wisdom. None of our inabilities are beyond His ability. So whatever your need, now or in the days ahead, 'Take it to the Lord in prayer.' None of our burdens are too heavy for Him. None of our depths will be beyond His reach. None of our troubles will be too troublesome for Him. As the Lord God Himself said to Abraham, when He promised a child to Sarah his wife when she was well beyond childbearing age: 'Is anything too hard for the LORD?' (Gen. 18:14). It was a rhetorical question. An anonymous writer took up the question in the following lines—lines which will surely help us on our way when we find ourselves living in difficult and discouraging days:

> Is the burden intolerable? Is the task impossible?
> Is the grief inconsolable? NOT WITH THE LORD.
>
> Is the darkness impenetrable? Is the sky un-pierceable?
> Is the tear un-dryable? NOT WITH THE LORD.
>
> Is the joy irrecoverable? Is the state irreversible?
> Is the case irretrievable? NOT WITH THE LORD.

Reflect on these points

1. *The God of the Bible is all-powerful. He is not subject to our human limitations and weaknesses. How we must beware of cutting him down to our size to make Him*

manageable, and of measuring Him by our own puny, human standards.

2. *God's people need never despair, for this omnipotent God condescends to hear the prayers of His children when they come to Him in need, and He then intervenes and gives both His saving and His sustaining grace.*

3. *No problem is too great for Him. No difficulty is insoluble to Him. No complexity is beyond His wisdom. None of our inabilities are beyond His ability. None of our burdens are too heavy for Him. None of our depths will be beyond His reach. None of our troubles will be too troublesome for Him.*

Approaching
a new year

Does the thought of a new year excite you or daunt you? Most of us have to confess that there is something about a time of change that unsettles us, as does the great 'unknown'. There is a verse in the Bible, though, that in its original setting of moving, changing times must have been a great help and comfort to those who heard it then, just as, if we let it grip our souls, it will be of great help and comfort to us as we approach the unknown year ahead. The words are contained in the second half of Isaiah 52:12, and they assure us that 'The LORD will go before you, and the God of Israel will be your rear guard.'

The God who goes before us

As we face the unknown year ahead, it is good to know the promise this verse contains: that 'the LORD will go before you'. Our God will pave our way. When we know God, having trusted in His Son, the Lord Jesus Christ, entering a new year is akin to entering the unknown in the arms of One who already knows everything that will ever happen, for He has 'foreordained whatsoever comes to pass' (Westminster Shorter Catechism, Question 7). We can even state that, when we have the eternal God as our loving heavenly Father, we are entering the New Year in the arms of the One who has already been where we are going. Our God is already there! In 2 Peter 3:8 we read, 'But do not ignore this one fact, beloved, that with the Lord one day is as a thousand years, and a thousand years as one day.' When we know God, we are safe in the arms of the One who has the key to the future, for He is the beginning and the end. In Revelation 1:8 God says of Himself, 'I am the Alpha and the Omega [that is, the first and last letters of the Greek alphabet] . . . who is and who was and who is to come, the Almighty.' The future will be sure to contain many surprises for us, but it holds no surprises for the eternal God, for He is all-knowing.

In the knowledge that our God is already in the future, we may, by faith, affirm that whilst we do not know our future, we do know the One who holds our future. We thus face the unknown future trusting in a known God: the God who has revealed Himself in the Scriptures and especially in the Saviour. He is too wise to make mistakes and too loving to be unkind. Here is our comfort:

> God holds the key of all unknown,
> And I am glad;
> If other hands should hold the key,
> Or if He trusted it to me,
> I might be sad.
>
> I cannot read His future plans;
> But this I know:
> I have the smiling of His face,
> And all the refuge of His grace,
> While here below.[1]

The God who is right behind us

Returning to our verse, notice that the Lord God is not only before us, but He is also right behind us: 'For the LORD will go before you, and the God of Israel will be your rear guard.' The 'rear guard' is actually a military term. It tells us of our divine protection. It speaks of God's constant presence through all the battles, dangers and difficulties we are sure to face in the coming days. Christians are not promised immunity from trouble, but we are assured of God's constant presence in and through our troubles. God promises, 'I will be with him in trouble' (Ps. 91:15), so that we will be able to testify, 'Though I walk in the midst of trouble, thou dost preserve my life' (Ps. 138:7). God's grace will always keep pace with whatever we face!

Knowing God, then, means facing changing times with One who does not change—One who is 'unchangeable, in His being, wisdom, power, holiness, justice, goodness, and truth' (Westminster Shorter Catechism, Question 4). 'For I the LORD do not change' (Mal. 3:6). 'Jesus Christ is the same yesterday and today and for ever' (Heb. 13:8). It is not strange, then, that the Bible often describes God as 'our rock'. A rock speaks of safety and stability. Whilst we will not be exempt from storms in the New Year, we may yet know God as our refuge within those storms.

> God is our refuge and strength,
>> a very present help in trouble.
> Therefore we will not fear though the earth should
>> change,

> though the mountains shake in the heart of the sea.
> (Ps. 46:1–2)

The Lord's our Rock, in Him we hide:
A shelter in the time of storm;
Secure, whatever ill betide:
A shelter in the time of storm.[2]

Both before us and behind us

The God of the Bible, then, is a God who both goes before us and is right behind us. What more could we ever want? 'For the LORD will go before you, and the God of Israel will be your rear guard.' Note the expression 'the God of Israel'. This gives us a glimpse of God's love for sinners, for Israel was no paragon of virtue—whether individually in the person of Jacob or collectively as a nation. God's love for sinners, of course, culminated in the sending of His own Son into the world to die to save them. And the salvation which Jesus procured at Calvary lasts way, way beyond the unknown year ahead! 'For I am sure that neither death, nor life, nor angels, nor principalities, nor things present, *nor things to come*, nor powers, nor height, nor depth, nor anything else in all creation, will be able to separate us from the love of God in Christ Jesus our Lord' (Rom. 8:38–39).

Happy New Year! And may you too know the blessing of the God who is both before us and behind us. Put your faith in Him. He alone knows the end from the beginning. By faith say, 'For I know whate'er befall me, Jesus doeth all things well.'

Before the hills in order stood,
Or earth received her frame,
From everlasting Thou art God,
To endless years the same.

A thousand ages in Thy sight
Are like an evening gone;
Short as the watch that ends the night
Before the rising sun.

Our God, our help in ages past,
Our hope for years to come;
Be Thou our guard while life shall last,
And our eternal home.[3]

Reflect on these points

*1. Our God will pave our way. When we know God,
    entering a new year is akin to entering the unknown in
    the arms of One who already knows everything that will
    happen, and, indeed, has already been where we are
    going. Our God is already there!*

*2. The 'rear guard' speaks of our divine protection: of
    God's constant presence through all the battles, dangers
    and difficulties we are sure to face.*

*3. The Bible often describes God as 'our rock'. A rock
    speaks of safety and stability. Whilst we will not be
    exempt from storms in the New Year, we may yet know
    God as our refuge within those storms.*

Divine sufficiency: the adequacy of God

In Psalm 121:2 we read, 'My help comes from the LORD, who made heaven and earth.' What a statement to take with us as we enter a new year! It is a statement and affirmation of divine sufficiency—of the all-embracing adequacy of God for His people's need; His sufficiency for our insufficiency; His adequacy for our inadequacy. The verse tells us that the same omnipotent power which God used to create the universe is actually available to help His people. Almighty God uses His omnipotence for the help and blessing of His people when they seek His aid. 'My help comes from the LORD, who made heaven and earth.' Psalm 146:5–6 echoes this thought when it says,

> Happy is he whose help is the God of Jacob,
>> whose hope is in the LORD his God,
> who made heaven and earth,
>> the sea, and all that is in them.

Matthew Henry, the famous Bible commentator, makes this apt pastoral comment on Psalm 121:2:

> We must encourage our confidence in God with
> this, that He 'made heaven and earth' and He
> who did that can do anything. He made the
> world out of nothing, Himself alone, by a word's
> speaking, in a little time and 'all very good', very
> excellent and beautiful; and therefore, how great
> soever our straits and difficulties are, He has
> power sufficient for our succour and relief.[1]

The God of the Bible is, then, as we have just seen, a God of divine sufficiency. The Bible reveals Him to be a God of both saving and sustaining grace.

The saving grace of God

The saving grace of God is manifested supremely in His Son, the Lord Jesus Christ. He is the all-sufficient Saviour of sinners. His death on the cross has procured our eternal salvation. By nature, we really are inadequate: we are sinners, unfit for God's presence, and under His wrath. Christ, however, is God's gracious provision—His all-sufficient provision—for the sinner's need.

The purpose of Christian preaching is to extol Christ's adequacy as Saviour to both sinner and saint, and to major constantly on His sinless life, atoning death, victorious resurrection, imputed righteousness and present intercession—His total sufficiency for our spiritual need. 'Jesus also suffered outside the gate in order to sanctify the people through his own blood' (Heb. 13:12). The blood of Jesus shed at Calvary sanctifies us. It sets us apart once and for all, for time and eternity, for God. It forgives our sins, it reconciles us to the Father, it declares us 'not guilty' and it makes us fit for heaven. 'Jesus alone' is the sinner's plea and the Christian's motto. He is our all-sufficient Saviour. His work on the cross was a perfect work of redemption. We cannot add anything to it, and nothing can be taken from it. His blood will never lose its power! The divine sufficiency of God is, then, revealed in His saving grace in Christ, for sinners.

The sustaining grace of God

The divine sufficiency of God is also revealed in the Bible by His sustaining grace which He imparts to His people. 'My help comes from the LORD, who made heaven and earth.'

In 2 Corinthians 12:9 God promises, 'My grace is sufficient for you.' This sustaining grace of God is revealed especially in times of trial. 'He giveth more grace as our burdens grow greater.[2] When trials come, God enables us to think biblically. He brings to our minds what we know about Him in His Word. His Word tells us that He is a sovereign God, in total control of all things. We remind ourselves that He is too kind to be cruel and too wise to make mistakes. We also remind ourselves of Romans 8:28: 'We know that in everything God works for good with those who love him, who are called according to his purpose.'

When trials come we may also know the special presence of God with us in and through the trial. He has promised never to fail us nor forsake us. He is with all His people, individually, by His Holy Spirit. The Greek word for the Holy Spirit is instructive. It is the word *Parakletos*, and it means 'one called alongside to help'. Some translate this as 'comforter', others as 'counsellor', 'encourager' or 'strengthener'. The Holy Spirit is all these to God's people. He is God's all-sufficient resource for us.

Remember, then, and prove the total adequacy of God as you face the future. Remember His saving and sustaining grace. Echo the psalmist's affirmation and say to yourself,

'My help comes from the LORD, who made heaven and earth.' He will most certainly prove to be more than adequate for your inadequacy and more than sufficient for your insufficiency. 'Now to him who by the power at work within us is able to do far more abundantly than all that we ask or think' (Eph. 3:20).

> The Lord is able to exceed
> And answer every cry
> His is our help in every need
> Our refuge ever nigh
> He's able to maintain His right
> His sovereignty make known
> To turn from darkness into light
> And seek and save His own
> He's able to subdue each foe
> Give victory to a worm
> Able to bear His people through
> And all His will perform
> He's able to remove our fears
> To show our sins forgiven
> To strengthen faith to dry our tears
> And make us fit for heaven
> He's able to preserve in peace
> And make us always blest
> From sin and sorrow to release
> And take us to His rest.[3]

Reflect on these points

1. *'Jesus alone' is the sinner's plea and the Christian's motto. He is our all-sufficient Saviour. His work on the cross was a perfect work of redemption. We cannot add anything to it, and nothing can be taken from it.*

2. *When trials come, God enables us to think biblically. He brings to our minds what we know about Him in His Word.*

3. *The Greek word for the 'Holy Spirit' means 'one called alongside to help', 'comforter', 'counsellor', 'encourager' or 'strengthener'. The Holy Spirit is all these to God's people. He is God's all-sufficient resource for us.*

God's listings

As a boy I used to love the *Radio Times*. In those days there were only two magazines which told you of the coming programmes on the TV and radio: the *Radio Times* and the *TV Times*. Now, many such magazines exist. I used to enjoy the *Radio Times* as much for its features as for deciding what would be good to view and listen to in the coming week.

Central to the *Radio Times* was its listings. These listings gave the times and brief details of scheduled programmes. However, these listings were not infallible, although they were followed in the majority of cases. A major news item, for instance, could oust a planned programme. Then, occasionally, there was industrial action by BBC workers or a power cut, resulting in a planned programme not being aired. I remember once my late dad looking forward to a programme on railways and sitting down ready to watch . . . but a power cut occurred at the exact moment the programme was due to start. What a disappointment!

The divine programme

Did you know that, according to the Bible, Almighty God has His *Radio Times*—that is, His series of planned events? These events have one goal, which is God's own glory and the blessing of His people. Unlike planned TV programmes, though, which may or may not go ahead, what God has planned will most surely come to pass, as He is Almighty God. Job confesses to Him in Job 42:2, 'I know that thou canst do all things, and that no purpose of thine can be thwarted.' In Isaiah 46:9–10 God pronounces,

> I am God, and there is no other;
>   I am God, and there is none like me,
> declaring the end from the beginning
>   and from ancient times things not yet done,
> saying, 'My counsel shall stand,
>   and I will accomplish all my purpose.'

Truly, Almighty God 'accomplishes all things according to the counsel of his will' (Eph. 1:11). In a nutshell, we are talking here about the eternal decrees of God.

The divine decrees

The Westminster Shorter Catechism is most helpful when it asks the question 'What are the decrees of God?' It answers in this way: 'The decrees of God are His eternal purpose, according to the counsel of His will, whereby, for His own glory, He hath foreordained whatsoever comes to pass' (Question 7).

Lawson's commentary elucidates this as follows:

> The decrees of God are His purposes, or what He has from eternity determined to do. And this answer tells us that God has so appointed everything that comes to pass. Nothing happens by change. Everything is arranged upon a plan, and that plan is the plan of God. He makes all things work together for good to them that love Him, and for evil to them that hate Him.[1]

Focus on the Christ

We see God's eternal programme being carried out in the Bible. This is especially so in relation to His Son, the Lord Jesus Christ. God revealed the details concerning His Son before He actually came to this earth to save His people. At the dawn of history, God promised that a descendant of Eve would come and crush Satan's head. Later on, He revealed that this Redeemer would be born of a virgin. He also revealed frequently that redemptive suffering was integral to His plan—that is, that the One He was going to send would suffer pain and punishment to redeem His people from the pain and punishment they deserved for their sins. So the sending of the Lord Jesus was part of God's programme—His eternal plan. Eventually, God executed His plan. 'When the time had fully come, God sent forth his Son, born of woman, born under the law, to redeem those who were under the law' (Gal. 4:4–5).

Focus on the Christian

The Bible also reveals that it is God's eternal programme that is being carried out when anyone comes to saving faith in Christ. Romans 8:30 explains that 'those whom he predestined he also called; and those whom he called he also justified; and those whom he justified he also glorified'. Salvation, then, is not haphazard. It is all according to God's divine plan. Specifically, here we see that it entails:

- *Predestination:* God chose His people in Christ before the foundation of the world.
- *Vocation:* those chosen in Christ in eternity past will

most surely be drawn to Christ in time. God will call them and draw them to the crucified Saviour.

- *Justification:* God, on the basis of Christ's work, declares the believer 'Not guilty'. Christ took our sin and guilt on the cross, and Christ clothes us with His perfect righteousness, and so makes us fit for heaven—which brings us to:

- *Glorification:* grace is glory begun; glory is grace completed. Glory is being in God's immediate presence. It is the consummation of bliss, resulting in our glorifying God and enjoying Him for ever.

So God has His eternal plan. And He cannot be frustrated in carrying out this plan, for the blessing of His people and the glory, honour and praise of His name.

How are we to respond to this? God's decrees elicit in us our great esteem and admiration of God. He is the sovereign God and worthy to be praised. God's decrees also humble us and cast us into the dust before Him. He is God. We are to submit to Him and His will. He does all things well. And if we belong to Jesus, God's decrees elicit our awe, wonder and humble and heartfelt thanks. Why should God choose us? Why should He save us? Why should He bestow on us eternal salvation? And, finally, God's decrees elicit our faith. He is the Lord God omnipotent. Despite appearances to the contrary, He has all things under His control. He is God Almighty—God Most High, the sovereign Ruler of the universe. He may be trusted through thick and thin.

Whate'er my God ordains is right:
His holy will abideth;
I will be still, whate'er He doth,
And follow where He guideth.
He is my God; though dark my road,
He holds me that I shall not fall:
Wherefore to Him I leave it all.[2]

Reflect on these points

1. *Almighty God has a series of planned events which have one goal: His own glory and the blessing of His people. And what God has planned will most surely come to pass.*

2. *God revealed the details concerning His Son before He actually came to this earth to save His people. The sending of the Lord Jesus was part of God's eternal plan.*

3. *It is God's eternal programme that is being carried out when anyone comes to saving faith in Christ. Salvation is not haphazard, but it is all according to God's divine plan.*

Peace: the lasting legacy of Jesus

A certain urban myth has two men at a funeral standing by the graveside of a mutual acquaintance. 'How much did he leave?' asks one. 'Everything!' replies the other. Joking apart, it is a reminder not to hold on too tightly to the temporal things of earth, for one day we will have to leave everything behind. 'We brought nothing into the world, and we cannot take anything out of the world' (1 Tim. 6:7).

Matthew Henry, the famous Bible commentator, said the following about the 'legacy' of the Lord Jesus Christ:

> When Christ was about to leave the world He
> made His will; His soul He committed to His
> Father; His body He bequeathed to Joseph of
> Arimathea; His clothes fell to the soldiers; His
> mother He left to the care of John. But what
> should He leave to His disciples that had left all
> for Him? Silver and gold He had none; but He left
> them that which is infinitely better, His peace.[1]

Peace of heart, soul and conscience is the lasting legacy of the Lord Jesus Christ to His followers. Among His final words to His disciples, Jesus said, 'Peace I leave with you; my peace I give to you; not as the world gives do I give to you. Let not your hearts be troubled, neither let them be afraid' (John 14:27). And the wonder of wonders is that you and I can be the beneficiaries of this blessed legacy of the Lord Jesus even today. For Jesus alone gives peace with God, and Jesus alone can impart the peace of God to the human soul.

Peace with God

Jesus gives us peace with God. Romans 5:1 reads, 'Therefore, since we are justified by faith, we have peace with God through our Lord Jesus Christ.' Colossians 1:20 describes Jesus as 'making peace by the blood of his cross'.

By nature, we are not at peace with God, for we are sinners by both nature and practice, and God is angry—even at war—with sinners. He cannot overlook the slightest infraction of His law. On the cross, however, Jesus dealt with our sin problem, and on our behalf paid the penalty for our breaking God's law. 'He himself bore our sins in his body on the tree' (1 Peter 2:24). When we put our faith in Jesus, believing that He died in our place, our sins are forgiven and the anger of God against us is appeased. Christians are at peace with God. We need not fear the wrath of God because Jesus, by His death on the cross, has averted it from us. 'He is the expiation for our sins' (1 John 2:2; 4:10).

Jesus' lasting legacy to His people, wrought by His atoning death, is, therefore, peace with God: complete pardon for our sins; a righteous standing with God where once we stood guilty before Him; and reconciliation with God where once we were alienated from Him. Jesus alone can give sinners peace with God. 'For he is our peace' (Eph. 2:14).

> Peace, perfect peace, in this dark world of sin?
> The blood of Jesus whispers peace within.[2]

The peace of God

The Lord Jesus is also able to impart the peace of God to

our souls. Whilst 'peace with God' refers to our standing—a standing which cannot be changed—'the peace of God' refers to our actual experience and state. According to Philippians 4:7, when we take our anxieties, cares and concerns to God in prayer, 'the peace of God, which passes all understanding, will keep your hearts and your minds in Christ Jesus'. Also, according to Galatians 5:22, 'the fruit of the Spirit is love, joy, *peace ...*'

Jesus imparts the peace of God to us by His Holy Spirit. He promised His disciples that He would send His Holy Spirit to them, and in due course His promise was fulfilled. The Holy Spirit—also known as 'the Comforter'—may be considered as the personal presence of the Lord Jesus with us day by day, through all the ups and downs and trials and tumults of our earthly pilgrimage. It was the Holy Spirit of God who caused the Scriptures to be written for our comfort, and the Holy Spirit is able to make the truth of God's Word real to us, and so give us God's peace—peace of heart and of mind—irrespective of, and unaffected by, the most stormy of earthly circumstances. He brings the comforting truths of God's Word to our minds—truths such as the following:

- *The absolute sovereignty of God:* He is on the throne, and has all things under His control.
- *The love of God:* This was demonstrated supremely and superlatively in the sending of His own Son to be our Saviour.

- *God's good and gracious providence:* He is working out all the details of our lives for our eternal blessing.
- *The eternal security of the soul united to Jesus:* Nothing in the present or the future will be able to separate or sever us from the love of God and the God of love.

Jesus, by His Holy Spirit and through His Word, is able to impart the peace of God to the human soul. Here is our anchor in the storm. Here is all-sufficient grace and help.

> Peace, perfect peace, with sorrows surging round?
> On Jesus' bosom nought but calm is found.
>
> Peace, perfect peace, our future all unknown?
> Jesus we know, and He is on the throne.[3]

Peace, then—both peace with God and the peace of God—is the lasting legacy of the Lord Jesus. And you too can be a beneficiary of this blessed legacy. The riches of Christ are just a prayer's breath away to all who call upon Him. Remember Jesus' words: 'Peace I leave with you; my peace I give to you; not as the world gives do I give to you. Let not your hearts be troubled, neither let them be afraid' (John 14:27).

> Peace in a troubled world, Jesus gives today
> Peace in a troubled world, peace that will not pass
>   away
> Shadows may deepen, and hopes grow dim
> Calm is the soul that is trusting Him
> Peace in a troubled world, Jesus gives today.[4]

Reflect on these points

1. *By nature, we are not at peace with God, for we are sinners. But when we put our faith in Jesus, believing that He died in our place, our sins are forgiven and the anger of God against us is appeased. Christians are at peace with God.*

2. *Jesus alone can give sinners peace with God: complete pardon for our sins; a righteous standing with God where once we stood guilty before Him; and reconciliation with God where once we were alienated from Him.*

3. *The Holy Spirit may be considered as the personal presence of the Lord Jesus with us day by day, through all the ups and downs and trials and tumults of our earthly pilgrimage.*

The friendship
of Jesus

There are friends who pretend to be friends,
> but there is a friend who sticks closer than a brother.

(Prov. 18:24)

Whatever uncertainties we may face in the days ahead, if we belong to Jesus one thing is certain: we can be sure of His faithful friendship. To the Christian, the friendship of Christ is a blessed reality enjoyed day by day, and which will continue for all eternity.

> There's not a friend like the lowly Jesus
> No, not one! no, not one!
> None else could heal all our soul's diseases
> No, not one! no, not one!
>
> *Jesus knows all about our struggles*
> *He will guide till the day is done;*
> *There's not a friend like the lowly Jesus*
> *No, not one! no, not one!*[1]

Let's consider further the blessed friendship of Christ:

1. *The Bible reveals a Christ who is infinite in His sympathy and understanding towards His own.* Hebrews 4:15 states this positive truth negatively when it says, 'For we have not a high priest who is unable to sympathize with our weaknesses, but one who in every respect has been tempted as we are, yet without sin.'

The God of the Bible is no remote deity, for in Christ He became man. He shared our human lot and plumbed our human depths. 'He was despised and rejected by men; a man of sorrows, and acquainted with grief' (Isa. 53:3). Charles Spurgeon, who knew something of both the darkness of this world and the Saviour's light, once said this about the Saviour's sympathy and understanding:

> 'God [is] with us' in our sorrows. There is no pang
> that rends the heart, I might almost say not one which
> disturbs the body, but what Jesus Christ has been with
> us in it all. Feel you the sorrows of poverty? He 'had
> not where to lay his head'. Do you endure the griefs
> of bereavement? Jesus 'wept' at the tomb of Lazarus.
> Have you been slandered for righteousness' sake,
> and has it vexed your spirit? He said 'Reproach hath
> broken mine heart.' Have you been betrayed? Do not
> forget that he too had his familiar friend, who sold him
> for the price of a slave. On what stormy seas have you
> been tossed which have not also roared about his boat?
> Never glen of adversity so dark, so deep, apparently so
> pathless, but what in stooping down you may discover
> the footprints of the Crucified One! In the fires and
> in the rivers, in the cold night and under the burning
> sun, he cries, 'I am with thee. Be not dismayed,
> for I am both thy companion and thy God.'[2]

This leads us to our second point:

2. *The Bible reveals a Christ who stands by His own.* He is indeed 'a friend who sticks closer than a brother'.

Matthew records that Christ's last words on earth to His disciples were 'Lo, I am with you always, to the close of the age' (Matt. 28:20). In the Upper Room, Christ promised, 'I will not leave you desolate [literally 'orphans']; I will come to you' (John 14:18). Jesus was referring here to the Holy Spirit, the third person of the Trinity. Christ is present with His people both individually and corporately in the person of His Holy Spirit. The Holy Spirit indwells every believer. 'Do you not know that your body is a temple of the Holy Spirit within you, which you have from God?' (1 Cor. 6:19). Whilst the presence of Christ and the person of the Holy Spirit are distinguishable in systematic theology, they are one and the same in Christian experience and reality. It is the person of the Holy Spirit who makes Christ real to us. Jesus explained how 'He [the Holy Spirit] will take what is mine and declare it to you' (John 16:15). The Holy Spirit then enables us to know and enjoy Christ's presence with us. In the words of the hymn to which we have already referred:

> There's not an hour that He is not near us
> No, not one! no, not one!
> No night so dark but His love can cheer us
> No, not one! no, not one!
>
> Did ever saint find this Friend forsake him?
> No, not one! no, not one!
> Or sinner find that He would not take Him?
> No, not one! no, not one![3]

It is the universal experience of Christians that Christ seems to draw nearer to us during times of trouble and distress. The pain of suffering is compounded by a sense of isolation and loneliness. We fear that we are in it on our own! But the Christian never suffers alone. In Christ we have a friend of infinite faithfulness. He stands by His people: 'He has said "I will never fail you nor forsake you"' (Heb. 13:5).

Finally:

3. *The Bible reveals a Christ who exerts His delivering power on behalf of His own.* In words that are well known, Jesus said, 'Greater love has no man than this, that a man lay down his life for his friends' (John 15:13). Christ did indeed lay down His life for His people. At Calvary, our Saviour 'gave himself for us to deliver us from the present evil age, according to the will of our God and Father' (Gal. 1:4).

The Christ of the Bible is 'mighty to save' (Isa. 63:1). Only His death at Calvary can deliver us from the fearful 'second death'. Only His blood has the potency to cleanse us from all sin and make us fit for heaven. Only His atoning work can reconcile the alienated sinner to God for time and eternity. At Calvary, in saving mercy, Christ exerted His saving power for His people's blessing and benefit when He 'loved the church and gave himself up for her, that he might sanctify her' (Eph. 5:25–26). At Calvary, Christ actually procured the salvation of His people. He is a Saviour who really saves!

It is also the common testimony of every Christian that

Christ still exerts His saving power from heaven for the relief of His people. 'This poor man cried, and the LORD heard him, and saved him out of all his troubles' (Ps. 34:6)—just as He did for Peter who, when on the Sea of Galilee, found himself 'afraid, and beginning to sink . . . cried out, "Lord, save me"' (Matt. 14:30). Proverbs 17:17 states that 'A friend loves at all times, and a brother is born for adversity.' In times of adversity, when all human props are unavailing, the friendship of Christ is especially proved.

When the Christian, like Peter, is 'afraid, and beginning to sink' on the stormy sea of this world, we have a Friend to whom we can turn. This Friend can still claim that 'All authority in heaven and on earth has been given to me' (Matt. 28:18). Jesus is well able to sustain us in our troubles. And the Lord Jesus, as the sovereign Lord of the universe, is even able to exert His power and providence so that our earthly troubles are removed, should He see fit. Truly, in the Lord of glory, seated at God's right hand, we have a Friend in the highest place, for whom no difficulty is too great, no trouble too deep and no problem too complex. Many times in Psalm 107 we read how God's Old Covenant people 'cried to the LORD in their trouble, and he delivered them from their distress' (Ps. 107:6 and throughout). The words can be fittingly applied in relation to Christians and their Saviour. The name 'Jesus' actually means 'the Lord delivers' or 'the Lord saves'. His name and His nature are thus inextricably bound.

'What a Friend we have in Jesus!' He is a friend of the utmost sympathy and understanding; His friendship is characterized by eternal, covenant faithfulness; and He possesses infinite saving power. So when our spirits are brought low through the wear and tear of this earthly pilgrimage, we may profitably mediate on the friendship which exists between us and our Saviour. Such a meditation on 'Jesus and His love' will surely be the needed tonic to revive our flagging souls, now and in the uncertain days ahead.

> There's no one like my Saviour;
> In seasons of distress
> He draws me closer to Him,
> To comfort and to bless;
> He gives me in temptation
> The strength of His right arm;
> His angels camp around me
> To keep me from all harm.
>
> There's no one like my Saviour;
> He pardons all my sin,
> And gives His Holy Spirit,
> A springing well within;
> He leads me out in service
> With gentle touch and mild;
> O wonder of all wonders
> That I should be His child.[4]

Soli Deo gloria.

Reflect on these points

1. *Christ is present with His people both individually and corporately in the person of His Holy Spirit. It is the person of the Holy Spirit who makes Christ real to us, who enables us to know and enjoy Christ's presence with us.*

2. *The Christian never suffers alone. In Christ we have a friend of infinite faithfulness who stands by His people.*

3. *When the Christian is 'afraid, and beginning to sink' on the stormy sea of this world, we have a Friend to whom we can turn. Truly, in the Lord of glory, seated at God's right hand, we have a Friend in the highest place, for whom no difficulty is too great, no trouble too deep and no problem too complex.*

Endnotes

Preface

1 J. Hart, 'How Good Is the God We Adore!'

Ch. 1 Celebrating a celebration?

1 Phillips Brooks, 'O Little Town of Bethlehem'.

Ch. 2 God in a manger

1 Edward Caswall, 'See, Amid the Winter's Snow'.

2 W. Gadsby, 'Ye Souls Redeemed with Jesus' Precious Blood'.

3 J. Hart, 'Come, Ye Redeemèd of the Lord'.

4 Cecil F. Alexander, 'Once in Royal David's City'.

Ch. 3 Light in the darkness

1 Charles Wesley, 'Let Earth and Heaven Combine'.

2 Phillips Brooks.

Ch. 4 Christmas jumpers

1 Edward Caswall.

2 Nicolaus Ludwig von Zinzendorf; translated by John Wesley.

Ch. 6 The first ever Christmas carol

1 Edward H. Bickersteth.

2 Nahum Tate, 'While Shepherds Watched Their Flocks by Night'.

Ch. 7 Taking on new things

1 J. Denham Smith, 'Rise, My Soul! Behold, 'Tis Jesus'.

2 Anon.

Ch. 8 Santa or the Saviour?

1 John Newton, 'Glorious Things of Thee Are Spoken'.

2 Augustus Toplady, 'Rock of Ages, Cleft for Me'.

3 Helen Howarth Lemmel, 'O Soul, Are You Weary and Troubled?'

Ch. 10 'Good King Wenceslas'

1 'Wenceslaus I, Duke of Bohemia', Wikipedia, https://en.wikipedia.org/wiki/Wenceslaus_I,_Duke_of_Bohemia.

2 Elizabeth R. Charles.

Ch. 11 The place of the Saviour's birth

1 J. C. Ryle, *Knots Untied* (London: William Hunt, 1874), p. 132.

Ch. 12 The royal birth

1 Phillips Brooks, 'O Little Town of Bethlehem'.

2 Charles Wesley.

Ch. 14 The original satnav

1 W. Chatterton Dix.

2 W. Chatterton Dix.

Ch. 15 A Christmas blessing

1 Charles Wesley, 'Hark! The Herald Angels Sing'.

Ch. 16 The unknown year ahead

1 John Parker.

2 Albert B Smith, 'I Do Not Know What Lies Ahead'.

Ch. 17 Fear not!

1 Augustus Toplady.

2 Tate and Brady, 'Through All the Changing Scenes of Life'.

3 William Gadsby, 'There Is an Overruling Providence'.

Ch. 18 God is in control

1 Maltie D. Babcock.

Ch. 19 A storm at sea

1 Anne R. Cousin, 'O Christ, What Burdens Bowed Thy Head!'

Ch. 20 One day at a time

1 Anon. (modernized from Old English).

2 D. W. Whittle.

Ch. 21 Big Ben

1 S. Wesley Martin.

2 W. F. Lloyd.

3 Charles Harrison Mason.

Ch. 23 The ultimate refuge

1 Corrie ten Boom's memoirs of her time in a concentration camp and her subsequent release are related in Corrie ten Boom, *The Hiding Place* (London: Hodder, 1976.

2 Vernon J. Charlesworth.

Ch. 24 Romans 8:28

1 William Cowper, 'God Moves in a Mysterious Way'.

Ch. 25 Divine omnipotence

1 Oscar C. Eliason.

2 Albert Midlane, 'Ever to the Saviour Cling'.

Ch. 26 Approaching a new year

1 Joseph Parker.

2 Vernon J. Charlesworth.

3 Isaac Watts.

Ch. 27 Divine sufficiency

1 Matthew Henry, *Commentary on the Whole Bible* (Peabody, MA: Hendrickson, 1991).

2 Annie Johnson Flint.

3 Author unknown.

Ch. 28 God's listings

1 Roderick Lawson, *Shorter Catechism with Comment and Scripture Proofs* (Belfast: Family Books, [n.d.]).

2 Samuel Rodigast; translated by Catherine Winkworth.

Ch. 29 Peace: the lasting legacy of Jesus

1 Matthew Henry, *Commentary on the Whole Bible* (Peabody, MA: Hendrickson, 1991).

2 Edward Henry Bickersteth.

3 Edward Henry Bickersteth.

4 J. W. Peterson, 'Oh What a Blessing to Know the Lord'.

Ch. 30 The friendship of Jesus

1 Johnson Oatman.

2 Charles Haddon Spurgeon, 'God With Us', from *Metropolitan Tabernacle Pulpit*, vol. 21, The Spurgeon Center, https://www.spurgeon.org/resource-library/sermons/god-with-us/#flipbook/.

3 Johnson Oatman.

4 Eliza E. Hewitt.